# Calculator Fun and Games

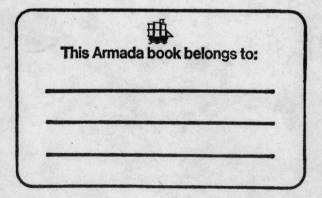

**This Armada book belongs to:**

BEN HAMILTON

# Calculator
# Fun and Games

*Illustrated by Bryan Reading*

An Armada Original

*Calculator Fun and Games* was first published in
Armada in 1981 by Fontana Paperbacks,
14 St James's Place, London, SW1A 1PS

© Ben Hamilton 1981

© Illustrations Fontana Paperbacks 1981

Printed in Great Britain by
The Anchor Press Ltd, Tiptree,
Colchester, Essex

# Contents

# Introduction

Calculators aren't new. Far from it. In fact, calculators of [some] kind have been around for thousands of years, although it has to be admitted that almost the only thing that modern electronic calculators have in common with their ancient predecessors is that they are still operated by human fingers. In nearly every other respect they are very different.

The earliest calculating machines sprang up in the great civilisations of the ancient world. These were counting frames on which there were beads which could be slid up and down wires. You may have seen pictures of these counting frames, and if you have you will probably know that they are called *abacuses*. *Abacuses* are very old, but even so they are still used by shop keepers and traders in many parts of the world today. These people have become very skilful at calculating quite difficult sums on their abacuses, and to see the beads flying up and down the wires and then hear the answer in a matter of seconds, you would think they had been using an electronic calculator.

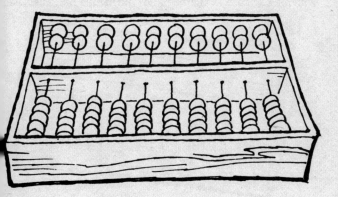

There is another quite old kind of calculating machin
still in current use, as well. This is the slide rule, which wa
invented by an English clergyman called William Oughtre
in the early part of the seventeenth century. He develope
two lines of numbers which could slide alongside each othe
and, by careful arrangement, could be used to solve mult
plication and division sums. His invention was develope
over the next two hundred years, and the modern slide ru
appeared at the beginning of this century.

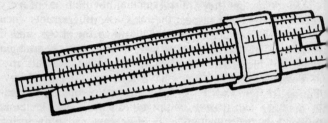

Perhaps one of the most remarkable calculating machin
of all time was invented by a young man of only ninetee
He grew up to become the great French mathematicia
Blaise Pascal. Pascal lived in the seventeenth century li
Oughtred. This was a time of major scientific developme
and Pascal made many important contributions to th
widening science of mathematics during his life. His calcu

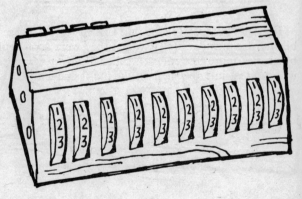

ating machine is no longer used today, but it is still an astonishing invention: it was the first digital calculator. The dials which show the numbers are driven by cog wheels that operate inside the box, rather like the mileometer that works inside the speedometer in a car.

In fact, most of the developments in calculating machines were based on Pascal's invention until the early years of this century, when the making of an electronic calculator became a real possibility.

You may remember that calculators used to be very expensive ten years ago. If you don't, ask your parents when they first saw an electronic calculator in the shops, and if they can remember how much it was. But over the past ten years the price of calculators has dropped dramatically. Today you see calculators everywhere, and the cost of buying one is now little more than the cost of buying a hardback book. The reason for this rapid spread of calculators is due to the fast-moving science of computer manufacturing and the growth of the famous 'silicon chip'.

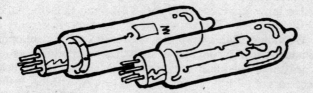

The early computers used parts called *valves*. These were big and frequently unreliable, but they were soon replaced by smaller, more efficient parts called *transistors*. Transistors were a great improvement on the old-fashioned valves, but

computers still needed thousands of them to do all the jobs and calculations they were expected to perform. So the scientists who designed computers tried to find a way of reducing the size of the transistors, both to make the computers smaller, and also to make them more efficient, because if the messages and signals inside the computers travelled less distance, they would be much quicker and more accurate. In the end they were able to produce tiny parts which contained over 1,000 transistors in a unit less than 5 mm wide. These are the *silicon chips*, and it is they which have brought about the micro-electronic revolution.

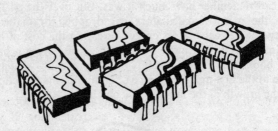

With silicon chips it is possible to make very efficient, very reliable and very small machines that can perform many times more complicated operations than their larger predecessors of twenty, or even ten years ago. And probably the greatest impact they have had on our everyday lives is the widespread use of pocket calculators, like the ones you can use to play all the games, answer all the puzzles and enjoy all the projects in this book.

Although nearly half the games in the book are for two or more players, in many cases you can be your own 'opponent', or play against the clock!

Modern calculators are a far cry from the early calculating machines, but they still require human brains to operate them. They may be able to do difficult sums far more quickly than we ever could imagine doing them ourselves, but they have to be shown how to do them. They cannot think for themselves. If you know how to use a calculator already turn to page 15 and get on with the games and other projects right away. If you don't, then read on.

As far as this book is concerned you will only need a calculator that displays eight digits in the calculator screen. (A digit is a single number from 0 to 9. All these digits appear on the calculator keyboard.)

Apart from the digits the only buttons that you will need to use are:

The four mathematical functions:  + plus
                                       − minus
                                       × multiplied by
                                       ÷ divided by

The equals sign:  =

The Clear sign which cancels an entry if you have made a mistake, or clears the screen for the next calculation. (This is usually marked C ALL, CLEAR, CA, C, or C/CE.)

And the ON/OFF switch, which you must switch to OFF whenever you finish using the calculator. If you leave it at ON, the batteries will quickly run down.

You use the calculator like this:

1. Switch from OFF to ON. A 0 will appear (you may need to press the CLEAR sign first).
2. Enter (that's to say, press) your first digit or number. If you are multiplying, adding, or subtracting this is the top number of the sum, if it is written down. If you are dividing this is the number you wish to divide.
3. Enter (press) the function key you want to use.
4. Enter (press) the other digit or number in the calculation.
5. Finally enter (press) the equals (=) key, and the answer will appear.
6. If you make a mistake, or if you want to start another calculation, press the CLEAR key and start again.
7. In some division sums in this book a dot will appear on the screen. This is the decimal point which you use with decimal fractions, but in most cases in this book you can ignore this.

# Fast Finger Figuring

This game is a test of both accuracy and speed. The object is to calculate a long, complicated sum on your calculator and finish with the correct answer, before your opponent finishes. However, if you finish first and have the wrong answer, and your opponent has the correct one, then he wins. So you have to be quick with your brain as well as with your fingers.

To play the game you will need:

    2 players
    2 calculators
    1 blackboard, or large sheets of paper
    1 thick pencil or pen, or chalk

This is how you play the game:

1. One player writes a long sum on the board using whatever numbers or mathematical signs he likes. But he does not write down what the answer to the sum is. The sum must be easily readable by both players.
2. Then both players stand two metres from each other with their calculators in their hands, switched 'off'.
3. One of them then shouts 'GO' and they both switch on their calculators and work out the sum as quickly and as accurately as they can.

15

4. The first player to get the answer shouts 'FINISHED', but he does not say what his answer is until the other player finishes. They check each other's answers, and if the player to shout 'FINISHED' is right he wins, but if he is wrong and the other player right, the other player wins.

5. The players play ten rounds to a game. The winner of the most rounds wins the game.

*Example:*

The written sum might be:

$3 \times 568 \times 89 - 342 + 401 \div 5 \times 218 - 67 \div 4320 \times 74 + 513 - 982$

One of the players shouts 'GO' and they both start to calculate.

The first player shouts 'FINISHED' with an answer of:

42284.81

The second player is slower, but he gets an answer of:

112838.47

They check the answers against the correct solution:

```
            3
         × 568
         ─────
          1704
          × 89
         ─────
        151656
         − 342
        ──────
        151314
         + 401
        ──────          30343
        151715 ÷ 5 ⟌ 151715
         30343
         × 218
        ──────
       6614774
```

16

$$6614774$$
$$- \ \ 67$$
$$\overline{6614707}$$

$$6614707 \div 4320$$

$$\begin{array}{r} 1531.1821 \\ 4320\overline{)6614707} \end{array}$$

$$\begin{array}{r} 1531.1821 \\ \times \ \ 74 \\ \hline 113307.47 \\ + \ \ 513 \\ \hline 113820.47 \\ - \ \ 982 \\ \hline 112838.47 \end{array}$$

Which means that the second player wins because he got the correct result. They play another nine rounds.

---

# Crafty Calculator Calculations

1. You can get the cubes of 3, 4, and 5 by adding the first two and the last two digits of the squares of 152, 251 and 237 respectively. (A *square* is a number multiplied by itself. A *cube* is a number multiplied by itself twice. The *square* of 2 is 4: $2 \times 2 = 4$. The *cube* of 2 is 8: $2 \times 2 \times 2 = 8$.)

This is how it works with 152:
Square 152 (multiply it by itself)

$$\begin{array}{r} 152 \\ \times \ 152 \\ \hline 23014 \end{array}$$

Take the first two and the last two
digits: 23 and 04, and add them

$$\begin{array}{r} 23 \\ + \ 04 \\ \hline 27 \end{array}$$

Now cube 3

$$\begin{array}{r} 3 \\ \times\ 3 \\ \hline 9 \\ \times\ 3 \\ \hline 27 \end{array}$$

The answers are the same, aren't they?

2. See what happens when you multiply 205128 by 4 on your calculator, then divide the answer by 4 and keep pressing × 4 and ÷ 4 one after the other.
The 8 keeps jumping from the front of the row of digits to the back, doesn't it?

3. You can get some interesting results by doing these multiplication sums. Try them on your calculator and see what you notice about the answers.

| | | |
|---|---|---|
| 2 × 8714 | 8 × 4973 | 78 × 624 |
| 2 × 8741 | 8 × 6521 | 87 × 435 |
| 3 × 4128 | 9 × 7461 | 75 × 231 |
| 3 × 4281 | 14 × 926 | 65 × 281 |
| 3 × 7125 | 24 × 651 | 65 × 983 |
| 3 × 7251 | 42 × 678 | 72 × 936 |
| 6 × 7251 | 51 × 246 | |

THEY'RE ALL DIFFERENT ?

# All or Nothing

In this game the object is either to reach an exact score of **21** yourself (*all*), or else to push your opponent's score *over* **21** so that he has *nothing*.

To play the game you will need:

2 players
1 calculator
2 pencils
1 sheet of paper

You play like this:

1. Toss a coin to decide who will start.
2. The first player chooses any digit (from 1 to 9), presses its key on the calculator and writes the digit down on the sheet of paper.
3. The second player adds any *other* digit by pressing the + sign on the calculator and then the key of the digit he has chosen. He also writes his digit down on the sheet of paper.
4. The first player takes his second turn by adding any digit which has not yet been used. He presses the + sign, presses the digit's key and writes the digit on the sheet of paper as before.
5. The game continues with each player choosing and adding a digit in turn, after checking on the sheet of paper that it has not been used before.
6. The play continues until one player brings the total to exactly **21**, or until one player pushes the score over **21**. The player who reaches **21** exactly wins outright. The player who pushes the score over **21** loses outright.
7. Play ALL OR NOTHING for ten rounds and the winner of the highest number of rounds is the overall winner of the match.

*continued*

*Examples:*

Player 1 presses 5 total = 5
Player 2 adds   6 total = 11
Player 1 adds   3 total = 14
Player 2 adds   7 total = 21

Player 2 wins

Player 1 presses 2 total = 2
Player 2 adds   6 total = 8
Player 1 adds   5 total = 13
Player 2 adds   4 total = 17
Player 1 adds   3 total = 20
Player 2 adds   1 total = 21

Player 2 wins

# Prime Number Premium

These are all the PRIME NUMBERS from 1 to 1000. PRIME NUMBERS are numbers which cannot be evenly divided by any other number. That is to say, they cannot be divided without leaving a remainder of some sort.

| | | | | | |
|---|---|---|---|---|---|
| 1 | 113 | 281 | 463 | 659 | 863 |
| 2 | 127 | 283 | 467 | 661 | 877 |
| 3 | 131 | 293 | 479 | 673 | 881 |
| 5 | 137 | 307 | 487 | 677 | 883 |
| 7 | 139 | 311 | 491 | 683 | 887 |
| 11 | 149 | 313 | 499 | 691 | 907 |
| 13 | 151 | 317 | 503 | 701 | 911 |
| 17 | 157 | 331 | 509 | 709 | 919 |
| 19 | 163 | 337 | 521 | 719 | 929 |
| 23 | 167 | 347 | 523 | 727 | 937 |
| 29 | 173 | 349 | 541 | 733 | 941 |
| 31 | 179 | 353 | 547 | 739 | 947 |
| 37 | 181 | 359 | 557 | 743 | 953 |
| 41 | 191 | 367 | 563 | 751 | 967 |
| 43 | 193 | 373 | 569 | 757 | 971 |
| 47 | 197 | 379 | 571 | 761 | 977 |
| 53 | 199 | 383 | 577 | 769 | 983 |
| 59 | 211 | 389 | 587 | 773 | 991 |
| 61 | 223 | 397 | 593 | 787 | 997 |
| 67 | 227 | 401 | 599 | 797 | |
| 71 | 229 | 409 | 601 | 809 | |
| 73 | 233 | 419 | 607 | 811 | |
| 79 | 239 | 421 | 613 | 821 | |
| 83 | 241 | 431 | 617 | 823 | |
| 89 | 251 | 433 | 619 | 827 | |
| 97 | 257 | 439 | 631 | 829 | |
| 101 | 263 | 443 | 641 | 839 | |
| 103 | 269 | 449 | 643 | 853 | |
| 107 | 271 | 457 | 647 | 857 | |
| 109 | 277 | 461 | 653 | 859 | |

*continued*

This is a way of turning the remainders in any division of a prime number into a positive advantage, because with only a few simple sums you can be sure of always ending up with 3, no matter which PRIME NUMBER you choose.

This is how it works:

1. Enter your prime number into the calculator.
2. Square it. That is, multiply it by itself.
3. Add 14. (a)
4. Divide the total by 12.
5. You will always end up with a remainder of 3.
6. To check this, multiply the number to the left of the decimal by 12 as well.
7. **This will always produce an answer which is 3 less than the first total at (a).**

| *Example:* | Try it with 829 | 829 |
| | Square it | × 829 |
| | | ——— |
| | | 687241 |
| | Add 14 | + 14 |
| | | ——— |
| | | 687255 |
| | | |
| | | 57271.25 |
| | Divide by 12 | 12⟌687255 |
| | Multiply 57271 by 12 | 57271 |
| | | × 12 |
| | | ——— |
| | | 687252 |
| | Subtract 687252 from 687255 | 687255 |
| | | − 687252 |
| | | ——— |
| | The remainder is 3 | 3 |

OH WELL— PERHAPS I'M PAST MY PRIME...

# Sum Square Surprises

There is something special about all of these squares of numbers. They are magic. In fact they are really called MAGIC SQUARES because they produce magic results. If you add the numbers in all the lines of digits, you will find that the answer will be the same in each case.

In this simple example the total of every line of digits is always 15:

|   |   |   |   |   |   |   |
|---|---|---|---|---|---|---|
| 8 | + | 1 | + | 6 | = | 15 |
| + |   | + |   | + |   |   |
| 3 | + | 5 | + | 7 | = | 15 |
| + |   | + |   | + |   |   |
| 4 | + | 9 | + | 2 | = | 15 |
| = |   | = |   | = |   |   |
| 15 |   | 15 |   | 15 |   |   |

Even the diagonals add up to 15 as well. Try it and see.

Now try these more complicated ones on your calculator. Try to find what the total for the lines of numbers should be in each of these:

| 16 | 3 | 2 | 13 |
|---|---|---|---|
| 5 | 10 | 11 | 8 |
| 9 | 6 | 7 | 12 |
| 4 | 15 | 14 | 1 |

= ?

| 17 | 24 | 1 | 8 | 15 |
|---|---|---|---|---|
| 23 | 5 | 7 | 14 | 16 |
| 4 | 6 | 13 | 20 | 22 |
| 10 | 12 | 19 | 21 | 3 |
| 11 | 18 | 25 | 2 | 9 |

= ?

*continued*

| 92 | 99 | 1 | 8 | 15 | 67 | 74 | 51 | 58 | 40 |
|----|----|-----|----|----|----|----|----|----|----|
| 98 | 80 | 7 | 14 | 16 | 73 | 55 | 57 | 64 | 41 |
| 4 | 81 | 88 | 20 | 22 | 54 | 56 | 63 | 70 | 47 |
| 85 | 87 | 19 | 21 | 3 | 60 | 62 | 69 | 71 | 28 |
| 86 | 93 | 25 | 2 | 9 | 61 | 68 | 75 | 52 | 34 |
| 17 | 24 | 76 | 83 | 90 | 42 | 49 | 26 | 33 | 65 |
| 23 | 5 | 82 | 89 | 91 | 48 | 30 | 32 | 39 | 66 |
| 79 | 6 | 13 | 95 | 97 | 29 | 31 | 38 | 45 | 72 |
| 10 | 12 | 94 | 96 | 78 | 35 | 37 | 44 | 46 | 53 |
| 11 | 18 | 100 | 77 | 84 | 36 | 43 | 50 | 27 | 59 |

= ?

| 46 | 81 | 117 | 102 | 15 | 76 | 200 | 203 |
|-----|-----|-----|-----|-----|-----|-----|-----|
| 19 | 60 | 232 | 175 | 54 | 69 | 153 | 78 |
| 216 | 161 | 17 | 52 | 171 | 90 | 58 | 75 |
| 135 | 114 | 50 | 87 | 184 | 189 | 13 | 68 |
| 150 | 261 | 45 | 38 | 91 | 136 | 92 | 27 |
| 119 | 104 | 108 | 23 | 174 | 225 | 57 | 30 |
| 116 | 25 | 133 | 120 | 51 | 26 | 162 | 207 |
| 39 | 34 | 138 | 243 | 100 | 29 | 105 | 152 |

= ?

| 16 | 41 | 36 | 5 | 27 | 62 | 55 | 18 |
|----|----|----|----|----|----|----|----|
| 26 | 63 | 54 | 19 | 13 | 44 | 33 | 8 |
| 1 | 40 | 45 | 12 | 22 | 51 | 58 | 31 |
| 23 | 50 | 59 | 30 | 4 | 37 | 48 | 9 |
| 38 | 3 | 10 | 47 | 49 | 24 | 29 | 60 |
| 52 | 21 | 32 | 57 | 39 | 2 | 11 | 46 |
| 43 | 14 | 7 | 34 | 64 | 25 | 20 | 53 |
| 61 | 28 | 17 | 56 | 42 | 15 | 6 | 35 |

= ?

AND DON'T FORGET THE DIAGONALS!

# Top Ten

In this game the players have ten goes. But their aim is to reach the highest score they can in those ten goes.

To play the game you will need:

  2 players
  2 calculators
  2 dice

You play like this:

1.  Both players roll the dice and the one with the highest total starts.
2.  The first player rolls the dice and enters his total on his calculator screen.
3.  The second player rolls the dice and enters his total on his calculator screen.
4.  The first player then rolls the dice again. This time if the total is an odd number he enters that on his screen. If it is even he multiplies by it.
5.  So the game continues with the two players taking it in turns to roll the dice, and they either multiply by their total, or else enter the total on their screens.
6.  When they have both had 10 goes, the one with the highest score is the winner with the TOP TEN.

*continued*

*Example:*

First player rolls the dice and gets 3 and 6 = 9.

First player enters 9 into his calculator.

Second player throws the dice and gets 1 and 6 = 7.

Second player enters 7 into his calculator.

First player rolls the dice and gets 5 and 2 = 7.

7 is an *odd* number so he enters that into his calculator = 97.

Second player rolls the dice and gets 4 and 6 = 10.

10 is an even number so he multiplies his total (7) by 10 = 70.

First player rolls the dice and gets 2 and 6 = 8.

8 is also an even number so he multiplies the total on his screen (97) by 8 = 776.

Second player rolls the dice and gets 5 and 4 = 9.

9 is an *odd* number so he enters that into his calculator = 709.

And so the game continues until both players have had ten goes and one has the TOP TEN.

---

# *Fill-in Puzzles*

Can you fill in the missing numbers from these sequences of numbers with the help of your calculator?

a.

$$1 \times 9 + 2 = 11$$
$$12 \times 9 + 3 = 111$$
$$? \times 9 + 4 = 1111$$
$$1234 \times ? + 5 = ?$$
$$? \times 9 + ? = 111111$$
$$123456 \times ? + ? = ?$$
$$? \times 9 + 8 = ?$$
$$12345678 \times ? + ? = ?$$

THE ANSWERS ARE AT THE BACK!

26

**b.**

$$1 \times 9 - 1 = 8$$
$$? \times 9 - 1 = 188$$
$$321 \times 9 - 1 = \ ?$$
$$? \times ? - 1 = 38888$$
$$54321 \times ? - ? = \ ?$$
$$? \times ? - ? = 5888888$$
$$7654321 \times ? - 1 = \ ?$$
$$? \times 9 - ? = ?88888888$$

**c.**

$$12345679 \times \ \ 9 = 111111111$$
$$12345679 \times 18 = 222222222$$
$$12345679 \times \ ? = 333333333$$
$$12345679 \times \ ? = 444444444$$
$$? \ \ \ \ \times 45 = 555555555$$
$$12345679 \times \ ? = \ ?$$
$$12345679 \times \ ? = 777777777$$
$$12345679 \times \ ? = 888888888$$
$$12345679 \times 81 = \ ?$$

What do you notice about the multipliers?
(Note: In this puzzle your calculator will show an overflow sign if it has only eight digits on the screen. Do not worry about this. Add the ninth digit by using the same one as the last digit on the screen.)

**d.**

$$9 \times 9 + 7 = 88$$
$$98 \times 9 + ? = ?88$$
$$9?7 \times ? + 5 = 8?88$$
$$987? \times 9 + ? = \ ?$$
$$98765 \times 9 + ? = 88888?$$
$$9876?? \times ? + ? = 8888888$$
$$??????3 \times 9 + 1 = ???????8$$
$$9876543? \times ? + 0 = 8????????$$

DO YOU COUNT WRONG ANSWERS?

27

# Odds and Evens

One of the players in this game tries to make the game end with an even number, while the other player tries to make it end with an odd number. The first player to start is the player who is trying to finish with the even number; the second player is the one who wants to end with an odd number.

To play the game you will need:

    2 players
    1 calculator
    1 pack of playing cards
    1 sheet of paper
    1 pencil

This is how you play:

1.  Each player draws a card from the pack. The player with the highest card is the first player (trying to end with an even number).
2.  The total of the two cards is entered into the calculator as the starting number. (In the game the royal cards all count as 10. The aces count as 1.)
3.  The players may only use the digits from 0 to 9 once each during each round. They may use them with any of the four mathematical functions ($+$, $-$, $\times$, $\div$), and they should use the paper and pencil to keep a check on those they have used.
4.  The only other restriction is that neither player is allowed to multiply or divide by 0.
5.  The round ends when both players have used all their digits.
6.  If the final result is an even number the first player wins, if it is an odd number the second player wins.
7.  If fractions occur, ignore the digits to the right of decimal point. Only the whole numbers count in this game.

*Example:*

| | |
|---|---|
| The first player draws 9 | The second player draws 6 |
| The total is entered into the calculator | 15 |
| First player adds 9 | + 9 |

$$24$$

| | |
|---|---|
| Second player divides by 8 | 3 |

$$8\overline{)24}$$

| | |
|---|---|
| First player multiplies by 6 | 3 |
| | × 6 |

$$18$$

| | |
|---|---|
| Second player subtracts 3 | − 3 |

$$15$$

| | |
|---|---|
| First player adds 7 | + 7 |

$$22$$

| | |
|---|---|
| Second player adds 5 | + 5 |

$$27$$

| | |
|---|---|
| First player multiplies by 2 | × 2 |

$$54$$

The game continues in this way until both players have used all their digits.

The first player can still use 1, 3, 4, 5, 8.
The second player can still use 1, 2, 4, 6, 7, 9.

# Marvellous Multiplications

Your calculator can provide hours of fun with multiplication sums, particularly as it takes out all the problem of having to work out the answers yourself.

Here are two examples of multiplication sums which produce marvellous results every time:

1. Did you know that if you multiplied 37037 by all the numbers between 3 and 27 it would give you six-digit answers which consisted of either the same three digits repeated, or of the same digit repeated six times? Look at these:

| 37037 | 37037 | 37037 | 37037 |
|---|---|---|---|
| × 3 | × 4 | × 5 | × 6 |
| 111111 | 148148 | 185185 | 222222 |

Every time you multiply by a multiple of 3 the answer is a row of the same digits. Now carry on yourself to 27.

2. Did you know that if you multiplied 15873 by the multiples of 7, you would end up with answers which produced rows of the same digit? Look at these:

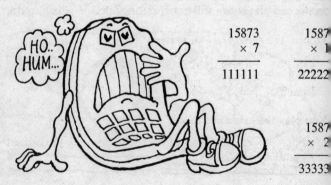

| 15873 | 1587 |
|---|---|
| × 7 | × 1 |
| 111111 | 22222 |

| 1587 |
|---|
| × 2 |
| 33333 |

30

And when you get above 7 × 10 (=70) the answers work like this:

$$
\begin{array}{r}
15873 \\
\times\ 77 \\
\hline
1222221
\end{array}
$$

Take the first and last numbers, add them together and put the result on the end of the row and you will have a complete sequence again: 1̸22222̸1̸

$$
\begin{array}{r}
1 \\
+\ 1 \\
\hline
2
\end{array}
$$

Put 2 on the end of 22222 and you get:  222222

Now try it yourself with the rest of the multiples.

---

# Sky High

The players in this game have to try to reach the highest score they can in ten goes. They may choose whether they multiply or add, so they have to look carefully at the numbers on the dice they have rolled before they decide which to do.

To play the game you will need:

- 2 or more players
- 2 calculators
- 2 pairs of dice
- 2 sheets of paper
- 2 pencils

You play the game like this:

1. Each player rolls a pair of dice. The one with the highest number goes first.
2. The first player rolls all four dice.

3. He looks at the four digits on the dice and decides whether he will arrange them in 2 two-digit numbers, which he will add together, or in 4 one-digit numbers which he will multiply together, to get the higest score he can.

4. He enters the total of whichever sum he chooses into his calculator and records it on his sheet of paper.

5. The second player now rolls the four dice and does the same.

6. The players take turns in this way until they have both had ten goes. After each go they add the new high number to their total, so that at the end the player with the highest total wins. Play the game for ten rounds, and the winner of the most rounds wins the match.

7. However, players must deduct 5 every time they roll the digit 5. They do this after using the four digits as usual.

*Example:*

Suppose that the first player rolls 5 3 6 2 on his first go, he can arrange the digits in one of these four ways:

$$53 + 62 = 115 \qquad 56 + 32 = 88$$
$$35 + 26 = 61 \qquad 52 + 63 = 115$$

or: $$5 \times 3 \times 6 \times 2 = 180$$

180 is the largest so he enters 180:  180
But there is also a 5 so he subtracts
5 as a penalty                        − 5
                                     ─────
                                      175

He then writes 175 on his sheet of paper.

On the next go he rolls 6 1 6 4, which he can arrange as:

$$61 + 64 = 125 \qquad 66 + 14 = 80$$
$$16 + 46 = 62 \qquad 64 + 61 = 125$$

$$6 \times 1 \times 6 \times 4 = 144$$

144 is the largest so he adds it to

$$\begin{array}{r} 175 \\ + \ 144 \\ \hline 319 \end{array}$$

and writes 319 on the sheet of paper – and so on, for ten rounds.

# The Magic 7 Trick

7 has always been a number with special magic powers. In this trick 7 is used to prove that the answers to any calculations carried out in this way are always the same – in fact the answers always end up as 7.

To perform this trick with your calculator this is what you must do:

1. Give the calculator to a friend and ask him to follow the instructions which you give him.
2. Tell him to enter any number into his calculator and write it down on a piece of paper. The number should be at least one digit less than the total number of digits that can be shown on the calculator screen.
3. Tell him to multiply by 2.
4. Tell him to add 5.
5. Tell him to add 12.
6. Tell him to subtract 3.
7. Tell him to divide the answer by 2.
8. Tell him to subtract the number he first entered.
9. Tell him the answer is 7. It will be.

For an extra dramatic effect tell your friend to cover the calculator screen while he is doing this trick. Then his surprise will be even greater when he looks at the result and sees that you are correct in your prediction.

Then try it again with a different number. *continued*

*Examples:*

Suppose your friend starts with a three-digit number, say 852

| | |
|---|---:|
| Enter 852 | 852 |
| Multiply by 2 | × 2 |
| | 1704 |
| Add 5 | + 5 |
| | 1709 |
| Add 12 | + 12 |
| | 1721 |
| Subtract 3 | − 3 |
| | 1718 |
| | 859 |
| Divide by 2 | 2)1718 |
| | 859 |
| Subtract the number first entered | − 852 |
| The answer will be 7 | 7 |

Now try with a larger number, say 753951.

| | |
|---|---:|
| Enter 753951 | 753951 |
| Multiply by 2 | × 2 |
| | 1507902 |
| Add 5 | + 5 |
| | 1507907 |

34

|                | 1507907 |
|---------------:|--------:|
| Add 12         | + 12    |

|                | 1507919 |
|---------------:|--------:|
| Subtract 3     | − 3     |

|                | 1507916 |
|---------------:|--------:|

|                         |           |
|------------------------:|----------:|
|                         | 753958    |
| Divide by 2             | 2/1507916 |
|                         | 753958    |
| Subtract the first number | − 753951 |

| Again the answer will be 7 | 7 |
|---|---|

# *Chicken*

People who call 'chicken' do so because they want to drop out of whatever they are doing because they are frightened of coming to harm. In this game the players have to avoid going over the limit of their calculators. Throughout the game their totals steadily increase until they eventually get very near the limit. The idea of the game is to make your opponent go over the limit but stay on the safe side yourself. And you are allowed one opportunity in the game to call 'chicken' and so miss that particular piece of addition.

To play the game you will need:

　2 players
　2 calculators. These must show the same number of digits on their screens.

You play like this:

1.　Both players enter three-digit numbers into their calculators. They cannot use the same digit twice and they cannot place 0 as the first digit.

2. The first player calls any digit (from 1 to 9) and they both multiply by this.
3. The second player then calls a one-digit number and they both multiply again.
4. At one time in the game either player may call 'chicken' which allows him to miss a turn, and so stay behind the other player.
5. It is also possible for a player to call a two-digit number whenever he thinks that he is safe, but the other player might be pushed over the limit by this sudden extra large calculation.
6. The first player to go over the limit of his calculator (when the overflow sign will show *or* the total will appear to drop) loses the game. The winner of five games wins the match.

*Example:*

| | | | |
|---|---|---|---|
| First player enters | 123 | Second player enters | 102 |
| First player calls 4 | × 4 | | × 4 |
| | 492 | | 408 |
| | × 6 | Second player calls 6 | × 6 |
| | 2952 | | 2448 |
| First player calls 8 | × 8 | | × 8 |
| | 23616 | | 19584 |
| First player calls | | Second player calls 15 | × 15 |
| 'chicken' and does | | | |
| not multiply | | | 293760 |
| First player calls 9 | 23616 | | 293760 |
| | × 9 | | × 9 |
| | 212544 | | 2643840 |

And so the game continues until one player goes over the overflow limit and loses the game. Of course the second player can still call 'chicken'; the first player cannot.

# Dotty Division

It might seem a bit pointless to do a division sum and eventually end up with the number you started with, but it's also one of the curious mathematical tricks which your calculator can demonstrate to you, if you give it a helping hand.

In this case your calculator will be able to give you an answer to the division of any three-digit number, which is the same as the number itself. All you have to do is to divide by 7, 11, and 13.

This is how you do it:

1. Think of any three-digit number and enter it into your calculator.
2. Now make a six-digit number by entering the first three digits in the same order.
3. Divide this number by 7.
4. Divide the answer by 11.
5. Divide this answer by 13.
6. Look at your answer and you'll see that it is the number you started with in the first place!

*Examples:* Imagine that you choose 572 as your number:

Enter it into your calculator            572
Make a six-digit number by repeating it    572572

Divide by 7               $\frac{81796}{7 \overline{)572572}}$

Divide by 11             $\frac{7436}{11 \overline{)81796}}$

Divide by 13             $\frac{572}{13 \overline{)7436}}$

The result is the same as the number you started with i.e.: *572*!

Try with another number, say 864:

| | |
|---|---|
| Enter it into your calculator | 864 |
| Make a six-digit number by repeating it | 864864 |

Divide by 7
$$\frac{123552}{7\,\overline{)864864}}$$

Divide by 11
$$\frac{11232}{11\,\overline{)123552}}$$

Divide by 13
$$\frac{864}{13\,\overline{)11232}}$$

Again, the result is the same as the original number. Now try it yourself. You can use any number from 100 to 999!

---

# Multiplication Puzzles

a.  Look carefully at these sums after you have calculated the answers on your calculator:

$8 \times 473 = ?$
$9 \times 351 = ?$
$15 \times 93 = ?$
$21 \times 87 = ?$
$27 \times 81 = ?$
$35 \times 41 = ?$

THEY'RE ALL NUMBERS?

What do they have in common?

b.  In these sums all nine digits are used to make multiplication sums and their answers. Before doing the sums on your calculator, can you work out what the answer might be?

| 1963 | 198 | 1738 | 159 | 138 |
|---|---|---|---|---|
| × 4 | × 27 | × 4 | × 48 | × 42 |

38

c.   Look carefully at these sums after doing them on your
calculator, and writing the answers on a piece of paper:

$1 \times 91 =$         $4 \times 91 =$         $7 \times 91 =$
$2 \times 91 =$         $5 \times 91 =$         $8 \times 91 =$
$3 \times 91 =$         $6 \times 91 =$         $9 \times 91 =$

What did you notice about the digits in the answers?
What did you notice about the digits in each of the answers
if you add them together?

d.   Using the digits 1, 3, 5, 7, 9, try to arrange them in a
number so that the number formed by the first two digits,
when multiplied by the number formed by the last two
digits, and with the digit in the middle subtracted from the
result, will give a row of the same digits. Keep a record of
your various attempts on a piece of paper so that you don't
get confused.

# The Word Game

Most people only use their calculators to do the sums they
can't do in their heads. How many bother to talk to their
calculators? You probably think that talking to a calculator
is a sign that you are going round the bend, but try dividing
7734 by 10,000 and see what your calculator says to you.
(You have to hold it upside down to read it.)

You see? With a little help from us, calculators can make
words of their own. Some of them have names, too. Enter

7718 and you'll see that the calculator is called ___ . Enter 53719 and the name ___ will appear on the screen. But in all these cases you have to hold the screen upside down to read what the calculator has written for you.

Although calculators can do sums far quicker than most of us can do them in our heads, they do not know as many words as we do. In fact they can only write nine letters, which is about a third of the number of letters in our alphabet. These are the numbers you have to enter in order to get the letters to appear:

To get B enter 8
To get E enter 3
To get G enter 6 (if you want a capital G enter 9)
To get H enter 4
To get I enter 1
To get L enter 7

To get O enter 0
To get S enter 5
To get Z enter 2

Of course you will have to remember to enter the numbers in reverse order to get the letters to appear right way round when you hold the calculator upside down.

These are some words which you can get your calculator to spell:

| 7738 | bell | 379919 | giggle | 0.0791 | igloo |
| 993 | egg | 5514 | hiss | | |

Try to spell these words with your calculator:

| bible | hole | legless | ooze | solo |
|-------|------|---------|------|------|
| glob | leg | oil | shell | zoo |

Now you understand how your calculator can help you communicate with your friends, here are some of the other calculator words which you can use. If you use a dictionary you will be able to find many others. Perhaps these will be words that you have never used before. If they are, then your calculator has taught you something new as well!

These are some names your calculator can spell:

| BESS | 5538 | BOBBIE | 318808 | LESLIE | 317537 |
|------|------|--------|--------|--------|--------|
| BILLIE | 317718 | ELSIE | 31573 | LILL | 7717 |
| BOB | 803 | LEO | 0.37 | | |

These are some common words:

| BEE | 338 | HOE | 304 | SIGH | 4615 |
|------|------|------|------|------|------|
| BEG | 638 | HOSE | 3504 | SIZE | 3215 |
| BIB | 818 | I | 1 | SLOSH | 45075 |
| BLESS | 55378 | ILL | 771 | SOB | 805 |
| BOBBLE | 378808 | ISLE | 3751 | SOIL | 7105 |
| BOGGLE | 376608 | LESS | 5537 | | |
| BOIL | 7108 | LIE | 317 | | |
| BOOHOO | 0.04008 | LOG | 607 | | |
| ELSE | 3573 | LOOSE | 35007 | | |
| GEESE | 35336 | LOSE | 3507 | | |
| GLEE | 3376 | LOSS | 5507 | | |
| GOBBLE | 378806 | OBOE | 3080 | | |
| GOES | 5306 | SEIZE | 32135 | | |
| GOOSE | 35006 | SELL | 7735 | | |
| GOSH | 4506 | SHE | 345 | | |
| HE | 34 | SHELL | 77345 | | |
| HIGH | 4614 | SHOE | 3045 | | |
| HILL | 7714 | SIEGE | 36315 | | |

# Last to One Million

The object of this game is to be the last player to reach on*
million on your calculator screen.

To play the game you will need

3 or more players
1 calculator for each player
dice

You play like this:

1. Each player enters a two-digit number into his calcu*
   lator. This can be any number, except that no digit may
   be used twice.
2. The players roll the dice to see who will start. The
   highest total begins, the second highest goes second, etc*
3. The first player then rolls the dice again twice. He car
   either *add* the totals to the number on his calculato*

screen, or he can *multiply* the number on the screen by *both* the totals, but he cannot mix the functions.

4. The second player now has his go, and so on.
5. No player may *add* for more than *five* goes in a row, so it is important to think carefully when to multiply and when to add. Bear in mind the whole time that you have to avoid reaching 1,000,000 before the others!

*Example:*

Player enters 36 into his calculator.
He rolls the dice and gets 12, so he starts.
He rolls the dice twice, getting 8 and 10.
He adds 8 to 36 = 44 and 10 to 44 = 54.
On the next throw he gets 7 and 9.
He adds 7 to 54 and gets 61 and 9 to 61 = 70.
On the next throw he gets 4 and 11.
He adds 4 to 70 = 74 and 11 to 74 = 85.
On the next throw he gets 4 and 3. These are quite low so he decides to multiply 85 by 4 = 340 and 340 by 3 = 1020. This means that he can now *add* for another five goes if he wants to.
If he had thrown 12 and 12, it would have been better to wait until the next throw before multiplying.

# Never Ending Nine

There are some sums in which one particular number never seems to want to go away. In this case the number is a single digit, 9. If you follow these instructions on your calculator you will quickly see that 9 will keep appearing at the end of your calculations, no matter how long you take in actually doing the sums.

To prove this fact, this is what you must do:

1. Enter any number of different digits into your calculator.

2. Note them on a piece of paper, or in your head.
3. Now press the subtract sign (−).
4. Enter the same digits, but this time in their reverse order.
5. Note the digits in your answer.
6. Add the digits together.
7. If the total has more than one digit, add these together and you will end up with 9.
8. What is more, your answer to the subtraction will be a multiple of 9 as well.

*Example:*

| | |
|---|---:|
| Try with a small number to begin with, say 76 | 76 |
| Press the subtraction sign (−) | |
| Enter the digits in their reverse order | −67 |
| | --- |
| The answer is 9 | 9 |

| | |
|---|---:|
| Now try with a larger number, say 5873 | 5873 |
| Press the subtraction sign (−) | |
| Enter the same digits in the reverse order | −3785 |
| | --- |
| | 2088 |

| | |
|---|---:|
| Add the digits in the answer | 8 |
| | 8 |
| | 2 |
| | + 0 |
| | --- |
| | 18 |

| | |
|---|---:|
| Add these digits | 8 |
| | + 1 |
| | --- |
| | 9 |

AND try dividing 2088 by 9 and you will see that it is a multiple of 9, like 18, as you would expect!

$$9\overline{)2088} \quad 232$$

44

# Snakes and Ladders

In the game of SNAKES AND LADDERS you move across the board sometimes sliding down the snakes and at other times climbing up the ladders. But eventually you reach the end of the board, don't you? Well, in this game, the process is exactly the same, except that instead of using a board, you use your calculator. And instead of using snakes and ladders, you use plus signs ($+$) and minus signs ($-$). The other major difference is that you play SNAKES AND LADDERS with somebody else, but you can play this game on your own.

The object of the game is to reduce any number up to six digits to 1 by either multiplying and adding, or by dividing. If your screen shows an odd number then you have to multiply; if it is even you have to divide. This is how it works:

1.  If the number you enter into your calculator is an odd number you must multiply by 3 and add 1.
2.  If it is an even number you must divide by 2.
3.  Look at the answer and repeat the operation, multiplying the odd numbers by 3 and adding 1, and dividing the even number by 2.
4.  See how many goes you will need to reduce the original six-digit number to 1.
5.  Some will come down very quickly, but others which you might think should come down quickly, in fact take a lot of goes before they reach 1.

*Example:*

Try with a fairly small number to begin with, say 35:

$$\begin{array}{r} 35 \\ \times\ 3 \\ \hline 105 \end{array}$$

Odd number so multiply by 3

*continued*

```
                                           105
Add 1                                     +  1
                                           ———
                                           106

                                            53
Even number so divide by 2             2/106
Odd number again so multiply by 3           53
                                          ×  3
                                           ———
                                           159
Add 1                                     +  1
                                           ———
                                           160
                                            80
Even number so divide by 2             2/160
                                            40
Even number so divide by 2             2/80
                                            20
Even number so divide by 2             2/40
                                            10
Even number so divide by 2             2/20
                                             5
Even number so divide by 2             2/10
                                             5
Odd number so multiply by 3               ×  3
                                           ———
                                            15
Add 1                                     +  1
                                           ———
                                            16
```

GULP!

Divide by 2 : will produce 1 after four more goes.

---

This is one of those rare numbers which provides a series of amazing, almost magical results when it is multiplied by a wide range of numbers.

Look what happens when you multiply it by 2, 5 and 6:

| 142857 | 142857 | 142857 |
|:---:|:---:|:---:|
| × 2 | × 5 | × 6 |
| 285714 | 714285 | 857142 |

What do you notice about the answers?

Now look what happens when you multiply it by 7:

$$142857 \times 7 = 999999$$

Curious, isn't it?

Try it with other numbers, two-digit ones, perhaps:

| 142857 | 142857 |
|:---:|:---:|
| × 13 | × 89 |
| 1857141 | 12714273 |

These numbers seem totally unalike, but try adding the digits at the beginning and the end and see what you arrive at.

Try multiplying this strange number by multiples of 7 that have two digits:

$$142857 \times 77 = 10999989$$

What do you notice about this in relation to the sums above?

Lastly, try multiplying the final answers to all the sums that do *not* use multiples of 7 by 7. And then divide them by 9 and see what you get.

You will see that 142857 is no ordinary number, and once you understand why it is not, try to multiply it to all sorts of numbers and enjoy the results that appear.

# All Digit Puzzles

a. These addition sums contain all the digits from 1 to 9.

```
   243          318          154
 + 675        + 654        + 782
 -----        -----        -----
   918          972          936
```

How many others can you find in which all nine digits appear? Write your answers down on a piece of paper to keep a check on your attempts.

b. Everyone knows that 1 plus 9 does not make 100. But it is possible to create sums on your calculator that use all the digits, by adding and multiplying, dividing or subtracting, to produce 100. Here is one example:

> I KNEW YOU COULD DO IT!

> WITH MY HELP

```
    123
  -   4
  -----
  (119)
  -   5
  -----
  (114)
  -   6
  -----
  (108)
  -   7
  -----
  (101)
  +   8
  -----
  (109)
  -   9
  -----
    100
```

How many others can you find? Use your calculator, but keep a written check of your efforts to avoid becoming confused.

c.   Can you use all the digits from 1 to 9 once each to form two numbers, one of which is twice the size of the other?

It sounds easy, but try it on your calculator and you'll find it takes some doing. Check your answer by multiplying your smaller number by 2.

d.   How many different multiplication sums can you form using all the digits on your calculator both in the multipliers and in the answers? Here are a few to get you started, but there are others as well for you to find:

$$
\begin{array}{r} 186 \\ \times\ 39 \\ \hline 7254 \end{array}
\qquad
\begin{array}{r} 483 \\ \times\ 12 \\ \hline 5796 \end{array}
$$

---

# *Pick and Choose*

This is a calculator game for both playing cards and calculators. It is also a game of choice. Both players have the option of either using the number on a hidden card or of using the corresponding key on the calculator, whichever will give them the higher number on their calculator screen. Of course, neither player will know what is on the hidden cards so there is a risk involved in choosing the hidden card. But that's what makes PICK AND CHOOSE so exciting, because the aim is to reach the highest total after 9 goes.

To play the game you will need:

  2 players
  2 calculators
  1 pack of playing cards                    *continued*

This is how you play:

1. Take all the cards above 9 from the pack. Leave the aces, however, because these count as 1's.
2. Shuffle the rest and place the first nine of them in three rows of three. These will correspond with the digit keys on the calculators and will be used in this order:

$$7 \quad 8 \quad 9$$
$$4 \quad 5 \quad 6$$
$$1 \quad 2 \quad 3$$

3. The cards should be placed face down so that neither player can see their values.
4. Each player now draws a card from the pack and places it face up.
5. The player with the higher card now chooses whether to use the hidden number on the first card in the nine (1) or whether to use the 1-digit key on his calculator.
6. The other player uses whichever the first player has left him.
7. They both enter their numbers into their calculators and then draw two more cards from the pack to decide who will go first in the next round.
8. Whichever player goes first now chooses between adding the hidden number on card (2) or else adding the 2 on the calculator keyboard. The other player takes whichever is left over.
9. The game continues in this way until all the nine cards have been used. The player with the highest total is the winner.
10. Obviously it is better to leave the lower numbers for the second player in the early rounds, but in the later ones, as the numbers get higher, you have to choose carefully as there is no knowing what the cards may hold beneath.

*Example:*

First player chooses the hidden card (1) and finds it
is valued at 8. He enters 8                                          8
The second player is left with 1             ·                         1
First player goes first again in the second round. He

chooses the hidden card and find it is valued 1 so
he adds 1 to 8 = 9                                             9
The second player is left with 2 – adds 2 to 1 = 3             3
And so it continues until 9.

---

# *Calculator Magic*

Ask your calculator to do these simple sums and it will give
you the date of the present year:

1.  Enter the date of the year you were born.
2.  Add to this the date of the year when you first went to
    school.
3.  Add to this total the age you will be at the end of this
    year.
4.  Add the number of years that have passed since you
    first went to school.
5.  Divide the total on your calculator screen by 2.
6.  The answer will be the date of this present year!

*Example:*

Imagine that you were born in 1970.
Enter 1970 into your calculator.
Imagine that you went to school in 1975, when you were 5.
Add 1975 into your calculator:         1970
                                     + 1975
                                     ———————
                                       3945        *continued*

51

Add your age at the end of 1981:

$$\begin{array}{r} 3945 \\ + 11 \\ \hline 3956 \end{array}$$

Add the number of years since you started going to school = 6:

$$\begin{array}{r} 3956 \\ + 6 \\ \hline 3962 \end{array}$$

Divide the total by 2 to get the date of this present year:

$$\begin{array}{r} 1981 \\ 2\overline{)3962} \end{array}$$

Your calculator can also miraculously give you your age and that of a friend of yours if you get it to do these simple sums:

1. Enter your age into the calculator.
2. Multiply it by 2.
3. Add 5.
4. Multiply the total by 50.
5. Add your friend's age.
6. Subtract 250
7. Divide the total by 100.
8. Press the equals key ( = ).
9. Magically, your age will appear on the left of the decimal point on the calculator screen and your friend's age will appear on the right!

*Example:*

Imagine that you are 11 years old.

Enter 11 into the calculator and multiply it by 2    = 22

Add 5                                                 +  5

$$\begin{array}{r} \hline 27 \end{array}$$

Multiply by 50                                        × 50

$$\begin{array}{r} \hline 1350 \end{array}$$

52

| Add your friend's age, say 9 | $+\ 9$ |
| --- | --- |
| | 1359 |
| Subtract 250 | $-\ 250$ |
| | 1109 |

$$\begin{array}{r} 11.09 \\ 100\overline{)1109} \end{array}$$

Divide by 100

Your age, 11, is on the left of the decimal point; your friend's age, 9, is on the right shown as 09!

---

# Up to Ten Thousand

The object of this game is to reach a score which goes as near to 9999 as it can without going over 10,000.

This is what you will need:

    2 players
    2 calculators

You play the game like this:

1. Both players enter any two-digit numbers into their calculators in secret, and then they press the divide key

$(\div)$. They can choose any two-digit number, but they must not use the same digit twice.

2. One player now calls any number between 1 and 9.
3. Both players enter this into their calculators and press the equals key $(=)$. Then they press the multiplication key $(\times)$.
4. The other player now calls any number between 1 and 9.
5. The game continues in this way with the players alternating between division and multiplication.
6. *But* after the first two rounds, the players are allowed to *add* a magic number. They do this by calling 'MAGIC NUMBER!' and reversing the first two digits of the total on the calculator screen. However, each player may only use a magic number twice in the game, so you have to choose carefully when to use them.
7. The player with the highest total after ten rounds is the winner.

*Example:*

| Player A<br>Enters 99 | Number chosen | Player B<br>Enters 74 |
|---|---|---|
| | Divide by 8 | |
| = 12.375 | | = 9.25 |
| | Multiply by 6 | |
| = 74.25 | | = 55.5 |
| | Divide by 2 | |
| = 37.125 | | = 27.75 |
| Magic number | | |
| = 73.125 | Multiply by 9 | |
| = 658.125 | | = 249.75 |
| | Divide by 3 | |
| = 219.375 | | = 83.25 |
| | Multiply by 7 | |
| = 1535.625 | | = 582.75 |
| | | Magic number |
| | | = 852.75 |

54

| Player A | Number chosen | Player B |
|---|---|---|
| | Divide by 1 | |
| = 1535.625 | | = 852.75 |
| | Multiply by 5 | |
| = 7678.125 | | = 4263.75 |
| | Divide by 4 | |
| = 1919.5312 | | = 1065.9375 |
| | Multiply by 9 | |
| = 17275.78 | | = 9593.4375 |

Player B wins because Player A went over 10,000!

---

# One Thousand and Eighty-Nine

If you want a clever trick to show your friends that you can work out sums even faster than a calculator, then memorize these rules and baffle them with your brilliance when you announce that the answer will always be 1,089.

This is what you have to do:

1. Give your friend a calculator and tell him to use it in such a way that you cannot see the screen.
2. Tell him to think of any three-digit number in which there is a difference of at least two between the first digit and the last.
3. Tell him now to reverse this number in his head.
4. Tell him to enter whichever of the numbers is the larger into the calculator.
5. Tell him to subtract the smaller number from this one.

6. Tell him to enter the addition sign (+).
7. Tell him to enter the answer to the subtraction in the reverse order of digits and to press the equals sign (=).
8. Tell him that the answer is 1,089 and get him to show you the screen to prove that you are correct.

*Example:*

| | |
|---|---|
| Imagine that your friend thinks of | 247 |
| Reverse the digits | 742 |
| 742 is the larger number so enter it into the calculator first | 742 |
| Subtract 247 | − 247 |
| | 495 |
| Enter the addition sign (+) | |
| Enter the answer in reverse order | + 594 |
| Press equals (=) | 1089 |

The answer is 1,089!

| | |
|---|---|
| Try with another number, say 698 | 698 |
| Reverse the digits | 896 |
| 896 is the large number so enter it into the calculator first | 896 |
| Subtract 698 | − 698 |
| | 198 |
| Enter the addition sign (+) | |
| Enter the answer in reverse order | + 891 |
| Press equals (=) | 1089 |

The answer will again be 1,089!

---

# Blind Sums

'blind' on their calculators, while the other player does the same sum correctly. The difference between the two answers is then awarded to the 'blind' player as his score. The first player to take his score over 50,000 loses the game.

To play the game you will need:

    2 players
    2 calculators
    2 sheets of paper
    2 pencils

You play the game like this:

1. Toss a coin to see who will play 'blind' first.
2. The 'blind' player hides his calculator under a piece of material so that he cannot see the keys, but is able to press them. Just to make sure, though, he must close his eyes as well.
3. The player who can see calls out any three-digit number and enters this into his calculator.
4. The blind player tries to enter the three-digit number into his calculator, too.
5. Then the player who can see calls one of the four mathematical functions ($+$, $-$, $\times$, $\div$), and both players enter this into their calculators, the blind player without looking.
6. The player who can see now calls out a two-digit number

which again they both enter, the blind player still without looking.

7. Finally, the player who can see calls out another mathematical function and a one-digit number, which they both enter.

8. The blind player looks at his calculator and they both press the equals (=) key.

9. The difference between the two totals is given to the blind player.

10. They change roles and the other tries to do the calculation 'blind' this time, in the same way. The first player to get a score of 50,000 is the *loser*.

*Example:*

| Player who can see calls 793 and enters this | | Blind player enters 482 | |
|---|---|---|---|
| Calls 'multiply', enters × | | Enters — | |
| Calls 58, enters 58 | | Enters 47 | |
| Calls 'add', enters + | | Enters × | |
| Calls 7, enters 7 | | Enters 4 | |
| Correct sum : | 793 | Incorrect sum : | 482 |
| | × 58 | | − 47 |
| | 45994 | | 435 |
| | + 7 | | × 4 |
| | 46001 | | 1740 |
| The difference is : | −1740 | | |
| | 44261 | | |

So the blind player's score after the first round is already very high! After a few games, though, you will become more familiar with the position of the keys.

# Ten High

This is a game using both dice and calculators. Each player has ten turns at rolling the dice and, depending on what he rolls, he performs one of four mathematical functions on his calculator. But the object of the game is to have a higher score after ten rounds than any of the other players.

To play the game you will need:

    3 or more players
    1 calculator per person
    Dice

This is how you play:

1. Toss a coin to see who starts.
2. In turn the players roll the dice and enter their totals into their calculators.
3. The first player rolls the dice again and then looks at this chart to see what he should do with his number:

    If he:    Rolls 2, add 2
              Rolls 3, enter 3 (no function)
              Rolls 4, multiply by 4
              Rolls 5, subtract 5
              Rolls 6, add 6
              Rolls 7, multiply by 7
              Rolls 8, subtract 8
              Rolls 9, add 9
              Rolls 10, enter 10 (no function)
              Rolls 11, divide by 11
              Rolls 12, multiply by 12

4. The second player then rolls the dice and consults the chart to see what he should do with his total.
5. Play continues in this way until all the players have rolled the dice ten times.
6. The player with the highest total on his calculator after ten goes is the winner.

*Example:*

| | |
|---|---:|
| Player rolls 7 on his first go and enters 7 | 7 |
| On his second roll he gets 4 and so multiplies | × 4 |
| | 28 |
| On his third roll he gets 9 and adds | + 9 |
| | 37 |
| On his fourth roll he gets 5 and subtracts | − 5 |
| | 32 |
| On his fifth roll he gets 8 and subtracts | − 8 |
| | 24 |
| On his sixth roll he gets 12 and multiplies | × 12 |
| | 288 |
| On his seventh roll he gets 10 and enters 10 | 28810 |
| On his eighth roll he gets 3 and enters 3 | 288103 |
| On his ninth roll he gets 2 and adds 2 | + 2 |
| | 288105 |
| On his tenth roll he gets 8 and subtracts | − 8 |
| | 288097 |

# Mixed Puzzles I

a. Look at any calculator keyboard and you will notice that 5 is always the digit in the middle. In this puzzle, you enter rows of different digits by pressing the three digit keys in any of the straight lines on the keyboard, but always going through 5 in the middle. Enter a row of three digits, then press the addition key (+) and enter the same row of digits in reverse. Press the equals key (=) and look at the answer. Now try with a different row of digits. You have eight to choose from.

What do you notice about these answers?
Why is this?

b.  Try multiplying 99 by any number from 1 to 100 on your calculator. Look carefully at the digits in the answers to these sums.
What do you notice about them?

c.  How can you make eight 8s add up to 1,000, when

$$
\begin{array}{r}
8 \\
\times\ 8 \\
\hline
64
\end{array}
$$

and 64 is 936 less than 1,000?

d.  What number will end up with the answer of 4 after you have added 8, subtracted 8, multiplied the answer by 8, and divided what you are left with by twice 4?

e.  Can you find a number through using your calculator, which is four digits long, and in which the last digit is double the first digit, the second digit is three less than the third digit, and the sum of the first digit and the last digit will be twice the third digit?

f.  How should you arrange the digits 1, 2, 3, 4, 5, 6, and 7 in their correct order to form an addition sum which will add up to 100?

g.   Can you think of three digits multiplied by 4 which will
give you an answer of 5?

h.   What is the answer to this sum:
          Half one half divided by one half?
(See if you can work it out in your head before doing it on
your calculator.)

---

# *Knock-out Calculator Trick*

You can stun your friends with your skill by using this trick.
You give a friend the calculator and tell him to follow your
instructions. Then at the end ask him for his result and
knock out the final digit in your mind. The number you will
be left with will be the number that he originally entered
into the calculator.

To perform the trick this is what you must tell your friend
to do:

1.   Tell him to enter any figure between 1 and 9,999,999.
2.   Tell him to multiply this by 3.
3.   Tell him to add 1.
4.   Tell him to multiply again by 3.
5.   Tell him to add the number he first entered.

6. Tell him to subtract 3.
7. Ask him to tell you the number on the calculator screen.
8. In your head knock out the last digit.
9. The number you are left with will be the number he first entered into the calculator.
10. Tell him the number, and tell him too that the odds were ten million to one that you would guess right. That should keep him quiet for a while.

*Examples:*

Suppose that your friend enters a number like 741852:

|                                                | 741852 |
| Multiply by 3                                  | × 3    |

|                                                | 2225556 |
| Add 1                                          | + 1     |

|                                                | 2225557 |
| Multiply by 3 again                            | × 3     |

|                                                | 6676671   |
| Add the number he first entered                | + 741852  |

|                                                | 7418523 |

| Ask him to tell you the result and knock out the last digit | 741852ƒ |

| The answer will be the number he first entered | 741852 |

| Try it with 357951                             | 357951 |
| Multiply by 3                                  | × 3    |

|                                                | 1073853 |
| Add 1                                          | + 1     |

|                                                | 1073854 |
| Multiply by 3                                  | × 3     |

|                                                | 3221562 |

*continued*

|  | 3221562 |
|---|---|
| Add the number he first entered | + 357951 |
|  | 3579513 |
| Ask him to tell you the result and knock out the last digit | 357951$\not{3}$ |
| The answer will be the number he first entered | 357951! |

---

# *Four of a Kind*

In this game eight digits from 1 to 9 are divided into ODD numbers and EVEN numbers, so that there are four of each kind. These are then given to the players, and they have five rounds in which to reach the highest score they can. The 'ODD' player takes the odd numbers 1, 3, 7, 9 while the 'EVEN' player has the even numbers 2, 4, 6, 8.

To play the game you will need:

  2 players
  2 calculators
  2 sheets of paper
  2 pencils

This is how you play:

1.  Toss a coin to see who will be ODD. ODD goes first.
2.  Each player chooses one of his numbers and enters it into his calculator.
3.  ODD then calls out one of the four mathematical functions ($+$, $-$, $\times$, $\div$).
4.  Both players press whichever key is called and then choose another of their numbers to perform this function. After this they press the equals key ($=$).

5. EVEN now calls one of the four functions and the players enter this and choose another of their remaining numbers, and then press the equals (=) key.
6. There are five rounds in the game and the player with the highest total at the end is the winner.
7. BUT each player may use each of his digits only once, AND each player may only call multiplication once in each round. So you have to choose carefully when to use the higher digits and when to choose to multiply.

*Example:*

| Odd enters 9 | | Even enters 6 | |
|---|---|---|---|
| Odd calls 'multiply' | | | |
| and chooses 7: | 9 | Enters 4: | 6 |
| | × 7 | | × 4 |
| | ——— | | ——— |
| | 63 | | 24 |
| | | Even calls 'add' | |
| Enters 3: | + 3 | Enters 2: | + 2 |
| | ——— | | ——— |
| | 66 | | 26 |
| Odd calls 'add' | | | |
| Enters 1 | + 1 | Enters 8 | + 8 |
| | ——— | | ——— |
| | 67 | | 34 |

Odd wins with the highest total.

THAT'S ODD!

# Doubling Up

Here is a set of fascinating calculator calculations which will enable you to double-up any three digit number just by performing two simple multiplication sums. When you press the equals key after the last one, the answer will flash up your original number on the screen, only this time it will be a six-digit number, with your original number appearing twice. It will have DOUBLED-UP.

This is how it works:

1. Enter any three-digit number.
2. Multiply it by 11.
3. Multiply it by 91.
4. Press the equals key and look at the answer.
5. Your original number will appear twice in the answer.
6. Now try it with another three-digit number. After all, you have from 100 to 999 to choose from!

*Examples:*

| | |
|---|---:|
| Try it with 101 | 101 |
| Multiply by 11 | × 11 |
| | ‾‾‾‾‾ |
| | 1111 |
| Multiply it by 91 | × 91 |
| | ‾‾‾‾‾‾ |
| | 101101 |

Now try it with 397

Multiply by 11

$$
\begin{array}{r}
397 \\
\times\ 11 \\
\hline
4367
\end{array}
$$

Multiply it by 91

$$
\begin{array}{r}
4367 \\
\times\ 91 \\
\hline
397397
\end{array}
$$

Now try it with 826

Multiply by 11

$$
\begin{array}{r}
826 \\
\times\ 11 \\
\hline
9086
\end{array}
$$

Multiply by 91

$$
\begin{array}{r}
9086 \\
\times\ 91 \\
\hline
826826
\end{array}
$$

Finally try it with the big one, 999

Multiply by 11

$$
\begin{array}{r}
999 \\
\times\ 11 \\
\hline
10989
\end{array}
$$

Multiply by 91

$$
\begin{array}{r}
10989 \\
\times\ 91 \\
\hline
999999
\end{array}
$$

You see it does work, doesn't it?

---

# *Middle Man*

The object of this game is to produce a final total which will fall between the totals of the two other players. You have to produce a sum which will give a total which is less than one of theirs and greater than the other. The player who succeeds in doing this is the MIDDLE MAN.

To play the game you will need:

| | |
|---|---|
| 3 players | 1 sheet of paper |
| 3 calculators | 1 pencil |

You play like this:

1. Each player thinks of a number between 1 and 15 and writes this down on the sheet of paper.
2. All three players look at the three numbers on the paper. They have to decide the best way in which they can use the three numbers and any two of the mathematical functions ($+$, $-$, $\times$, $\div$) to produce a total that will fall between those of the other players.
3. The three numbers can be used in any order and any *two* mathematical functions can be used. But the skill lies in trying to guess what results the others will produce.
4. The first player to be MIDDLE MAN ten times is the winner.

*Example:*

The three figures on the paper might be:  13
                  6
              10

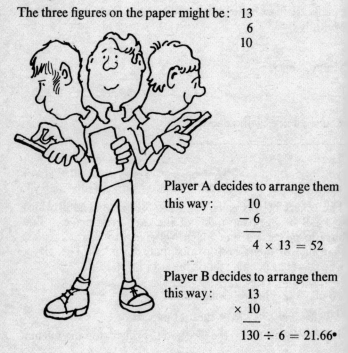

Player A decides to arrange them this way:

$$10$$
$$\underline{-\ 6}$$
$$4 \times 13 = 52$$

Player B decides to arrange them this way:

$$13$$
$$\underline{\times\ 10}$$
$$130 \div 6 = 21.66\bullet$$

68

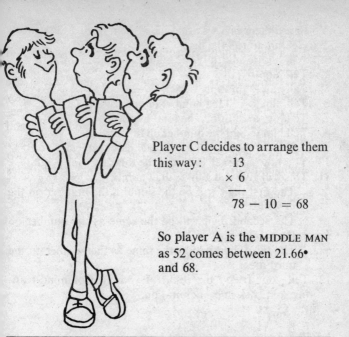

Player C decides to arrange them
this way:      13
            × 6
          ―――
          78 − 10 = 68

So player A is the MIDDLE MAN
as 52 comes between 21.66•
and 68.

# Calculator Mind Reading

Here's a marvellous way of using your calculator to help
you perform a breath-taking feat of magical skill that will
astound your friends and convince your parents that you
can't be as bad at Maths as they thought.

To perform this trick you will need:

    3 dice
    1 friend
    1 calculator

This is what you do:

1.   Give your friend the dice and the calculator and tell him

to use them in a way that hides them from your sight.
2. Get him to roll the dice.
3. Ask him to multiply the number on the first die by 2.
4. Tell him to add 3.
5. Tell him to multiply by 5.
6. Tell him to add the number on the second die.
7. Tell him to multiply the total by 10.
8. Tell him to add the number on the third die.
9. Ask him for the total on the calculator screen.
10. You now subtract 150 from the total, in your head.
11. This will give you a three digit number:
    The first digit will be the same as the number on the first die.
    The second digit will be the same as the number on the second die.
    The third digit will be the same as the number on the third die.
12. Tell your friend the result of your feat of mind-reading, and bask in his admiration.


*Example:*

Imagine that the dice show 5 3 6

| | |
|---|---:|
| Multiply the first number by 2 | 5 |
| | × 2 |
| | 10 |
| Add 3 | + 3 |
| | 13 |
| Multiply by 5 | × 5 |
| | 65 |
| Add the number on the second die: 3 | + 3 |
| | 68 |
| Multiply by 10 | × 10 |
| | 680 |

Add the number on the third die: 6          + 6

                                              686
As for the total (686) and subtract 150    − 150

                                              536

Tell him the dice he rolled showed 5  3  6!

_____

# Some Sum!

And now for something completely different . . . a quiz and
a calculation combined! All you have got to do is answer
the questions, perform the sums and come up with the right
answer – which you can check on page 120.

1.  Multiply the year of the Battle of Hastings by a 'baker's
    dozen'.
2.  Multiply the answer by the number of days in a leap
    year.
3.  Now subtract the number of days .in an ordinary
    February.
4.  Divide the answer by the number of years in a millen-
    nium.
5.  Subtract two plus twice two from the total.
6.  Now subtract the date of the Battle of Hastings.
7.  Divide the total by the number of years a centenarian
    has lived.
8.  Subtract the number of steps in the title of a novel by
    John Buchan – and what's the answer you've got?

COULD YOU
REPEAT
THAT?

71

# Some Square Sums!

If you multiply a number by itself, this process is called SQUARING in mathematics, as you no doubt know. With a calculator, squaring any number is a piece of cake. You can do it in two ways, usually:

1.  Enter the number into the calculator. Press the multiplication key (×). Enter the number again. Press the equals key (=) to get your answer.
2.  An easier way on many calculators is to enter the number into the calculator. Press the multiplication key (×) TWICE. Press the equals key (=) to get your answer.

Here is an interesting formula, using this principle, which will enable you to start with the square of an odd number, square two other numbers, do a subtraction sum and end with the square you started with. Sounds complicated?
This is how it works:

1.  Enter any odd number into the calculator.
2.  Square it.
3.  Find the two consecutive numbers which make this square when they are added together.
4.  Square these two numbers.
5.  Subtract the smaller from the greater.
6.  The difference between them will be the same as the square of the original number you started with.

Look at this example to see the working in action:

| | |
|---|---:|
| Choose an odd number, say 19 | 19 |
| Square it | × 19 |
| | ——— |
| | 361 |

Find the two consecutive numbers
by dividing the answer by 2 and
taking the whole numbers on either

$$\begin{array}{r} 180.5 \\ 2\overline{)361} \end{array}$$

The whole numbers are 180 and 181

Square 180

$$\begin{array}{r} 180 \\ \times\ 180 \\ \hline 32400 \end{array}$$

Square 181

$$\begin{array}{r} 181 \\ \times\ 181 \\ \hline 32761 \end{array}$$

Subtract the lesser from the greater

$$\begin{array}{r} 32761 \\ -\ 32400 \\ \hline 361 \end{array}$$

The answer is the same as the square of 19, the square you started with.

Now try it yourself with other odd numbers.

# *Lowest of the Low*

High scores and huge numbers have no place in this calculator game. The object here is to end the game with the lowest score possible.

To play the game you will need:

2 or more players
1 calculator for each player (though you can play with only one calculator between you).
1 pair of dice
1 sheet of paper for each player
1 pencil for each player

This is how you play:

1. Each player enters 50 into his calculator.
2. Toss a coin to decide who will start.
3. The first player rolls the dice, adds the digits and then compares his total with the chart below:
   If his total is:
   2 he must divide the total on the calculator by 2.
   3 he must multiply the calculator total by 2.
   4 he must subtract 4 from the calculator total.
   5 he must add 5 to the calculator total.
   6 he must multiply the calculator total by 3.
   7 he must divide the calculator total by 3.
   8 he must subtract 8 from the calculator total.
   9 he must add 8 to the calculator total.
   10 he must multiply the calculator total by 2.
   11 he must divide the calculator total by 2.
   12 he must subtract 12 from the calculator total.
4. The other players take their turns, checking their dice totals with the chart and carrying out the required operations.
5. Each player may choose to *pass* once only during the game.
6. The game lasts for ten rounds. The player with the lowest total on his calculator is the winner.

*Example:*

Imagine that the first player rolls 5
to begin with. He looks at the chart and
sees that he must add 5 to his 50

$$
\begin{array}{r}
50 \\
+ 5 \\
\hline
55
\end{array}
$$

On his next go he rolls 8, and must
subtract 8

$$
\begin{array}{r}
- 8 \\
\hline
47
\end{array}
$$

On his next go he rolls 2 and must
divide by 2

$$23.5$$
$$2\overline{)47}$$

On his next go he rolls 10 and must
multiply by 2

$$\begin{array}{r} 23.5 \\ \times\ 2 \\ \hline 47.0 \end{array}$$

On his next go he rolls 9 and must
add 8

$$\begin{array}{r} +\ 8 \\ \hline 55 \end{array}$$

On his next go he rolls 5 and must
add 5

$$\begin{array}{r} +\ 5 \\ \hline 60 \end{array}$$

And so his game continues for another four rounds. If his
score is lower than that of any other player then he will
be the winner.

75

# The Three-Two-Zero Trick

This trick of magical, mental arithmetic relies on the subtraction of a magic number, 320. This is the number you have to use to reduce your friend's calculator total to the number which he has been using as the basis of his calculations. After all his calculator sums, you will be able to tell him the number that he started out with, although you will have seen none of his calculations.

To perform this trick this is what you will have to do:

1. Tell your friend to enter any number up to six digits long.
2. Tell him to multiply this by 2.
3. Tell him to add 4.
4. Tell him to multiply by 5.
5. Tell him to add 12.
6. Tell him to multiply by 10.
7. Ask him to tell you the result showing on the calculator screen.
8. All you have to do is subtract the magic number, 320.
9. Now forget about the last two digits.
10. The number you are left with will be the number your friend first entered into the calculator.
11. Announce this with justified pride and absolute confidence, but whatever you do DON'T give away the secret.

*Examples:*   Suppose your friend entered 46795          46795
              Multiply by 2                            × 2
                                                    ───────
                                                     93590

|                                   |          |
| --------------------------------- | -------: |
|                                   |    93590 |
| Add 4                             |      + 4 |
|                                   |    93594 |
| Multiply by 5                     |      × 5 |
|                                   |   467970 |
| Add 12                            |     + 12 |
|                                   |   467982 |
| Multiply by 10                    |     × 10 |
|                                   |  4679820 |
| Ask for the result and subtract 320 |   − 320 |
|                                   |  4679500 |

Forget the last two digits.
The answer is the number your
friend began with.

4679500

|                                   |          |
| --------------------------------- | -------: |
| Try it with 786512                |   786512 |
| Multiply by 2                     |      × 2 |
|                                   |  1573024 |
| Add 4                             |      + 4 |
|                                   |  1573028 |
| Multiply by 5                     |      × 5 |
|                                   |  7865140 |
| Add 12                            |     + 12 |
|                                   |  7865152 |
| Multiply by 10                    |     × 10 |
|                                   | 78651520 |
| Ask for the result and subtract 320 |   − 320 |

Forget the last two digits.
You see, it works again!

78651200!

# Best of Ten

In this game the two players have ten rounds in which each must try to reach a higher total on his calculator than the other player.

To play the game you will need:

  2 players
  2 calculators
  Dice

You play like this:

1.  Both players roll one die each and enter the number they have rolled into their calculators.
2.  The first player rolls his die again and calls out any of the four mathematical functions ($+$, $-$, $\times$, $\div$).
3.  Both players then use this function with whatever number he rolled.
4.  They now look at the totals on their caculator screens.
5.  If the total is a prime number (one that cannot be evenly divided by any other) then the player must multiply his total by that number.
6.  If the total is a number which can be evenly divided by 2 then the player must multiply by 2.
7.  If the total is a number which can be evenly divided by 3 then the player must subtract 3.
8.  If the total is a number which can be evenly divided by 5 then the player must add 5.
9.  When both players have completed their sums, the second player rolls his die and calls any of the four mathematical functions.
10. Both players then carry out this sum and look again at their totals.
11. They do their own sums again and then according to the rules above.

12. And so the game continues for another eight rounds.
13. The player with the highest total is the winner.

*Example:*

| Player A | Player B |
|---|---|
| First rolls 4 | First rolls 2 |
| He enters 4 into his calculator | He enters 2 into his calculator |
| He then rolls 6 | |
| He calls 'multiply by 6': | He multiplies 2 × 6: |

```
      4                        2
    × 6                      × 6
   ____                     ____
     24                       12
```

24 is divisible by 2 and 3, but choosing 2 is best because you must multiply by 2:

12 is divisible by 2 and 3, but 2 is best because you must multiply by 2:

```
     24                       12
    × 2                      × 2
   ____                     ____
     48                       24
```

The play continues in this way with Player B rolling next and calling the function, and then Player A taking his second turn, until both players have had five turns and there have been ten rounds altogether.

I WAS DOING ALL RIGHT 'TILL MY BRAIN BROKE DOWN

# Snap Calculations

Everyone knows the card game called SNAP. You have to try to match identical cards, don't you? Well in this set of calculations you perform three simple multiplication sums and end up with matching numbers at either end of the answer.

This is how it works:

1. Enter any number into your calculator up to 999.
2. Multiply it by 7.
3. Multiply it by 11.
4. Multiply it by 13.
5. Look at the result.
6. If your original number was a single-digit number, then it will appear twice, at either end of the answer.
7. If it was a two-digit number, then it will appear twice separated by a 0.
8. If it was a three-digit number, then it will appear twice, side by side.
9. In every case though, from 1 to 999, the number you have chosen will flash up on the screen as a matching pair, just like the winning cards in SNAP.

*Examples:*

| | |
|---|---:|
| **Single-digit number, say 7** | 7 |
| **Multiply by 7** | × 7 |
| | 49 |
| **Multiply by 11** | × 11 |
| | 539 |
| **Multiply by 13** | × 13 |
| | 7007 |

| | |
|---|---:|
| Two-digit number, say 83 | 83 |
| Multiply by 7 | × 7 |
| | ――― |
| | 581 |
| Multiply by 11 | × 11 |
| | ――― |
| | 6391 |
| Multiply by 13 | × 13 |
| | ――― |
| | 830830 |
| | |
| Three-digit number, say 914 | 914 |
| Multiply by 7 | × 7 |
| | ――― |
| | 6398 |
| Multiply by 11 | × 11 |
| | ――― |
| | 70378 |
| Multiply by 13 | × 13 |
| | ――― |
| | 914914 |

# Calculator Poker

Poker is a very popular card game. It was the game that all the cowboys played from Dodge City to the Mexican border in the famous casinos and saloons of the Wild West. Now it is possible to play a form of poker that uses calculators instead of playing cards. The aim of the game is the same – you have to try to end with the best *hand*. You can work out which is the best at the end of each game just by looking at the chart.

To play Calculator Poker you will need:

   2 or more players
   1 calculator per player
   paper
   pencils

This is how you play:

1. Each player enters any four-figure number into his calculator. The number should be chosen at random, but 0's are not allowed.
2. Each player presses the multiplication key ( × ) and then passes his calculator to the player on his left.
3. The calculator screens must be covered when they are passed around, so that the players cannot see what their neighbours have entered. Once they have been passed, each player enters another random four-figure number, without looking at the screen and without using any 0's.
4. The calculators are then passed back. The owners press the equals keys ( = ) and look at the answers which appear.
5. The seven digits on the right of the screen form the playing 'hand'.
6. The players have to choose the five digits which will give them the best 'hand' from their choice of seven.
7. In CALCULATOR POKER 0's count as tens, and therefore they are the highest numbers.
8. Once all the players have selected their hands, they look at the chart and decide who has the best hand, and is therefore the winner.
9. The highest scoring 'hands' are the top of the chart, the lowest scoring at the bottom. The winner with the best 'hand' gets one point. The first player to get ten points is the winner.

## The Chart of hands

| | |
|---|---|
| Five of the same kind (all the numbers the same) | eg. 55555 |
| Straight Flush – even (five different even numbers) | eg. 42806 |
| Straight Flush – odd (five different odd numbers) | eg. 19753 |
| Four of the same kind | eg. 38333 |
| Full House (three of one number and two of another) | eg. 69699 |
| Flush (all even numbers) | eg. 48462 |

Flush (all odd numbers)                    eg. 59737
Straight (five numbers in sequence)        eg. 34567
Three of the same kind                     eg. 21711
Two pairs                                  eg. 63613
One pair                                   eg. 65895

If there is a tie, the *highest number* wins.

---

# Ten Total Trick

In this calculator trick your friend will be busily carrying out your instructions on the calculator, while all you have to do at the end is to count the number of tens in the answer to find the number he started with.

This is what you must do:

1.  Tell your friend to enter any number up to seven digits long into the calculator.
2.  Tell him to multiply it by 3.
3.  Tell him to add 2.
4.  Tell him to multiply again by 3.
5.  Tell your friend to add the number which is 2 greater than the number he first entered.
6.  Ask for the answer.
7.  Count the number of tens in the answer and that will give you the number he started with.
8.  Tell him what the number he started with was. And quickly change the subject, before he has a chance to ask you something which you might not be able to answer!

*Examples:*

| | |
|---|---:|
| Suppose your friend entered 1873659 | 1873659 |
| Multiply by 3 | × 3 |
| | 5620977 |
| Add 2 | + 2 |
| | 5620979 |
| Multiply by 3 | × 3 |
| | 16862937 |
| Add the number which is two greater than 1873659, ie: 1873661 | + 1873661 |
| | 18736598 |

Ask him to tell you the answer and count the number of tens (that is, all the digits to the left of the last digit)
The answer is
– the number he first entered.

1873659

| | |
|---|---:|
| Try it with a smaller number, say 8574 | 8574 |
| Multiply by 3 | × 3 |
| | 25722 |
| Add 2 | + 2 |
| | 25724 |
| Multiply by 3 | × 3 |
| | 77172 |
| Add the number which is two greater than 8574, ie: 8576 | + 8576 |
| | 85748 |

Count the number of tens =
the number he first entered!

8574

# Mixed Puzzles II

a. Fill in the missing numbers in this sequence:

$$? \times 3367 = 111111$$
$$? \times 3367 = 222222$$
$$99 \times 3367 = 333333$$
$$132 \times ? = 444444$$
$$165 \times 3367 = ?$$
$$? \times 3367 = ?$$
$$? \times 3367 = 777777$$
$$264 \times 3367 = ?$$
$$? \times 3367 = ?$$

b. What two numbers multiplied together will give you the prime number 7? Think carefully.

c. Which three consecutive numbers add up to 27?

d. How many whole numbers can you show on the screen of an eight digit calculator? This is a sum, don't try to enter them all one after another.

e. Fill in the missing digits in this sequence:

$$15873 \times 7 = 1?????$$
$$15873 \times ?? = 222222$$
$$15873 \times ?? = 333333$$
$$158?? \times 2? = ??4???$$
$$????3 \times ?? = 555555$$
$$15873 \times ?2 = 666666$$
$$????? \times 49 = ??????$$
$$15873 \times ?6 = 88888?$$
$$15873 \times ?3 = 9?????$$

f. Fill in the missing digits in this sequence:

$$1 \times 8 + 1 = ?$$
$$12 \times 8 + 2 = ??$$
$$1?? \times 8 + ? = 987$$
$$1??? \times 8 + 4 = ???6$$
$$1???? \times 8 + 5 = ????5$$
$$1????? \times 8 + ? = ?????4$$
$$1?????? \times 8 + ? = ???????3$$
$$1??????? \times 8 + ? = ????????2$$

I'M JUST WORKING OUT WHAT PAGE THE ANSWERS ARE ON

PAGE 122 ACTUALLY

# Over and Out

You probably know that there are six balls in an OVER in cricket. Well, in this game you do not have balls to bowl, but you have six goes on the calculator instead. The object of the game is to be OUT, in other words to get down to 0 in your six goes.

To play the game you will need:

Yourself
1 calculator

You play the game like this:

1. Enter any six-digit number into your calculator. You may not use 0 and no digit may be used twice.
2. Now, in six goes you have to try to reduce your number to 0.
3. You are allowed to use any two-digit number you like in each go, and you can use any of the four mathematical functions ($+$, $-$, $\times$, $\div$).
4. It may seem obvious to keep dividing and subtracting, but sometimes it is better to add a number in order to produce a total which can be cleanly divided by another two-digit number.
5. Once you have mastered reducing your figure to 0 in six goes, try bringing it to 0 in five and even four goes!

*Example:*

Imagine that you start with a six-digit number like:

583621

Add 19

$$583621$$
$$+ \quad 19$$
___
$$583640$$

88

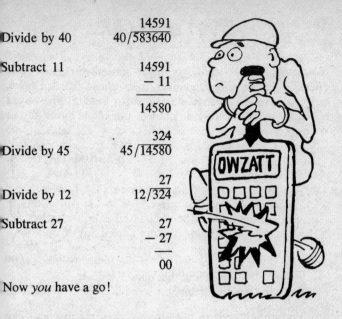

| | |
|---|---|
| Divide by 40 | $\dfrac{14591}{40\,/\,\overline{583640}}$ |
| Subtract 11 | $\begin{array}{r} 14591 \\ -\ 11 \\ \hline 14580 \end{array}$ |
| Divide by 45 | $\dfrac{324}{45\,/\,\overline{14580}}$ |
| Divide by 12 | $\dfrac{27}{12\,/\,\overline{324}}$ |
| Subtract 27 | $\begin{array}{r} 27 \\ -\ 27 \\ \hline 00 \end{array}$ |

Now *you* have a go!

---

# Neighbouring Numbers

The idea of this game is to get the highest score out of a total of six rounds to win the game. The skill of the game lies in carefully choosing the digits in each round, because in this game the players have a choice of using the keys only immediately neighbouring the ones they choose.

To play the game you will need:

    2 players
    2 calculators
    2 sheets of paper
    2 pencils

This is how you play:

1. Toss a coin to decide who is going to start.
2. The first player calls one of the four mathematical functions $(+, -, \times, \div)$ after both have cleared their calculator screens and entered one digit of their choice.
3. The second player then uses one of the numbers to the right or the left of his chosen number to perform the function. If the chosen number is on the edge of the keyboard then there is only one number to choose. If it is in the middle column there are two numbers from which to choose.
4. The second player then calls one of the mathematical functions and the first player has to use this with one of the numbers on either side of his chosen number.
5. After the first player has completed his calculations, they both press their equals keys $(=)$ and the player with the highest total wins. If the totals are the same, neither player wins and the round is a draw.
6. The player with the highest score after ten rounds wins the game.
7. The players are only allowed to use each number once during the game.
8. Each player may only say 'add' and 'subtract' twice and 'multiply' and 'divide' three times.

*Example:*

First player enters 9

First player says 'divide'

Second player enters 5

Second player can choose 4 or 6. He chooses 6:

$$6\overline{)5}\phantom{x} \begin{array}{r} 0.83\bullet \\ \hline \end{array}$$

Second player says 'subtract'

First player can only choose 8 as 9 is on the edge:

$$\begin{array}{r} 9 \\ -8 \\ \hline 1 \end{array}$$

The second player wins the round because 1 is larger than 0.83•.

The next nine rounds continue, but the first player cannot use 9 again and cannot say 'divide' more than once more. The second player can still say 'divide' twice and can still use 9, which might be to his advantage.

---

# The Age Trick

You can use your calculator to amaze your friends by accurately guessing their age, without in fact seeing any of the calculations that make up the trick. All you have to do is to give them the calculator and then ask them to do all the operations themselves. In the end they will tell you the answer and you will tell them how old they are. It's as simple as that.

This is how you do it:

1. Give your friend the calculator. (Tell him to hide the screen from your view and to enter his age on it.)
2. Tell him to multiply his age by 2.
3. Tell him to add 1.
4. Tell him to multiply the total by 5.
5. Tell him to add 5.
6. Tell him to multiply this total by 10.
7. Tell him to subtract 100.
8. Ask him to tell you the answer.
9. All you have to do is to drop the last two digits and the ones that you are left with will be the same as your friend's age.
10. Tell him and amaze him with your intelligence and the accuracy of your calculator.

*Example:*

Suppose that your friend is 12 years old.
He enters 12 into the calculator.

| | |
|---|---:|
| Then he multiplies by 2 | 12 |
| | × 2 |
| | —— |
| | 24 |
| He adds 1 | + 1 |
| | —— |
| | 25 |
| He multiplies by 5 | × 5 |
| | —— |
| | 125 |
| He adds 5 | + 5 |
| | —— |
| | 130 |
| He multiplies by 10 | × 10 |
| | —— |
| | 1300 |
| He now subtracts 100 | − 100 |
| | —— |
| | 1200 |

He tells you the answer is 1200
You eliminate the last two digits 12ØØ
And you tell him that he is 12 years old.

(A word of warning. Ladies over a certain age become very secretive about their age. Either they may not tell you the truth in the first place, or, worse still, they might tell you the truth and then be furious when you loudly announce that they are really fifteen years older than everyone else imagined them to be. Be careful!)

92

# Two Thousand and One

This is a useful game to keep tucked up your sleeve for those odd moments when you have nothing to do, and no one else to do it with – because you can play this game all by yourself. All you are trying to do is to reach 2001 in as few goes as possible.

To play the game you will need:

    1 calculator
    1 pack of playing cards

You play like this:

1.  Remove the royal cards from the pack (King, Queen and Jack).
2.  Begin the game by taking any two cards from the pack and adding their values.
4.  Enter the total on to your calculator screen.
5.  Now draw out two more cards. One of these will be the number you next enter into the calculator, the other will tell you whether you multiply, divide, add, or subtract with it. You can choose which card does which.
6.  The game continues by drawing two cards at a time and increasing your total on the calculator screen. But remember that the aim is to reach 2001 in as few goes as possible.
7.  If you find that you have used all the cards without reaching 2001 reshuffle them and carry on.

These are the mathematical functions which go with the numbered cards in the pack:

| | | | |
|---|---|---|---|
| 1 (ace) and 10 | any function | 4 and 8 | ÷ |
| 2 and 6 | × | 5 and 9 | + |
| 3 and 7 | − | | |

*Example:*

Draw 6 and 4. Add them = 12
Draw 3 and 2
Either: subtract 2 (3 = −)
Or: add 3 (2 = +)
Adding is better, so add 3 = 15
Draw 10 and 6
Either: add 10 (6 = +)

Or: multiply by 6 (10 = any function)
$$15 + 10 = 25$$
$$15 × 6 = 90$$
Multiplying is better, so multiply by 6
Carry on drawing, and make sure that you increase your total as quickly and as efficiently as you can.

---

# *Nine Nonsense*

Did you know that any number can be evenly divided by 9? 'Nonsense,' you will say. 'How can any number be evenly divided by 9? It's impossible.'
It isn't, however. Look at this simple set of rules and you will see how it can be done on your calculator.

This is what you must do:

1. Enter any number into your calculator. It can have two digits, or it can have eight, it does not matter, as long as there are more than one.
2. Make a note of the digits in the number, either in your head, or on a piece of paper.

3. Press the subtraction key (−).
4. Now enter another number that uses the digits you first entered, but in any order. The only thing you have to watch is that the second complete number is smaller than the one you first entered.
5. Complete the subtraction sum by pressing the equals (=) key.
6. Now divide the answer by 9 and you will find that it will be evenly divided. That is, there will be no remainders left over (or figures after the decimal point).
7. When you have worked through this successfully once, try it with another number, perhaps a larger to prove that it really works in any case.

*Examples:*

| | |
|---|---:|
| Start with a small number, say 953 | 953 |
| Note the digits used | |
| Press the subtraction key (−) | |
| Enter another, smaller number using the same digits | − 593 |
| Press the equals (=) key | 360 |
| | 40 |
| Divide by 9 | 9⟌360 |

There are no remainders!

| | |
|---|---:|
| Now try with a larger number, say | 76184 |
| Note the digits used | |
| Press the subtraction key (−) | |
| Enter another, smaller number using the same digits | −41786 |
| Press the equals key (=) | 34398 |
| | 3822 |
| Divide the answer by 9 | 9⟌34398 |

There are no remainders in this case, either!

# Above and Below

In this game you can win by either getting the highest score above 0, or by getting the lowest minus score below 0. Both plus and minus numbers count in this game.

To play the game you will need:

   3 or more players
   1 calculator per player
   sheets of paper
   pencils

You play like this:

1. Each player enters any two-digit number into his calculator. It can be either a plus number or a minus number.
2. Each player then writes down the number on his calculator screen and its sign (+ or −), and passes the paper to the player on his right.
3. The players again write down their numbers on their calculator screens with their signs, this time below the number written on the sheet of paper.
4. They continue to pass the sheets of paper round to the right, until each player has written his sign on every sheet of paper, and the papers have returned to their owners.
5. The players have to make a sum using the numbers in the order in which they appear on the sheet, so that they can end up with the highest plus or minus number. However, each player is only allowed to use multiplication once in the sum.
6. The player with the largest number wins the round. There are ten rounds to a game. The player who wins the greatest number of rounds is the winner.

*Example:*

A list of numbers might look like this:
$$-48$$
$$+97$$
$$+26$$
$$-38$$

You could either multiply by + 97:
$$-48 \times + 97 + 26 - 38 = -4668$$

Or by + 26:
$$-48 + 97 \times + 26 - 38 = +1236$$

Or by − 38:
$$-48 + 97 + 26 \times - 38 = -2850$$

So, clearly, multiplying by + 97 would give the largest number in this round.

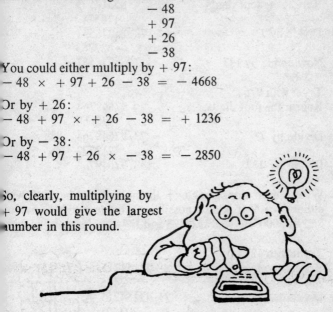

# Even Division

Your calculator probably has a screen which can display eight digits in a row. If it has, then you can use all that space to do these amazing divisions and produce an even answer, with no remainders (or decimal fractions), every time.

Provided that you repeat the first four digits of the number to make your eight-digit number you will be able to divide it evenly by 73 and 137 – both of which look very awkward numbers at the best of times!

*Examples:*

Try it with 8531:

| Repeat the four digits | 85318531 |
| | 1168747 |
| Divide by 73 | 73 / 85318531 |
| | 622763 |
| Now divide by 137 | 137 / 85318531 |

Try it with 9764:

| Repeat the four digits | 97649764 |
| | 1337668 |
| Divide by 73 | 73 / 97649764 |
| | 712772 |
| Divide by 137 | 137 / 97649764 |

What is even more amazing is that if your number ends with either 0 or 5, it is also possible to divide it evenly by 365 and by 50005, as well as by 73 and 137!

Try it with 4215:

| Repeat the four digits | 42154215 |
| | 577455 |
| Divide by 73 | 73 / 42154215 |
| | 307695 |
| Divide by 137 | 137 / 42154215 |
| | 115491 |
| Divide by 365 | 365 / 42154215 |
| | 843 |
| Divide by 50005 | 5005 / 42154215 |

In each case the eight-digit number can be evenly divided by these odd numbers!

WHAT A LOT OF DIGITS!

# Out in Ten

In this game players start with three-digit numbers on their calculator screens and try to reach 0 exactly in ten goes by performing different mathematical operations.

To play the game you will need:

2 players
2 calculators
2 sheets of paper
2 pencils

This is how you play:

Both players enter three-digit numbers into their calculators, making sure that they do not repeat any digits.
The first player calls one of the four mathematical functions ($+$, $-$, $\times$, $\div$).
Each player enters one digit (from 0 to 9) in secret. But they write the digits down on their sheets of paper. The second player now calls one mathematical function. Both players enter this and then choose another of the digits from 0 to 9. However, each digit may only be used *once* in each game by each player. And the players are not allowed to multiply by 0 after the middle of the game (the fifth round).
The players must remember all the time that the aim is to reach 0 exactly after ten rounds. They have to choose their digits and mathematical functions very carefully. For, if any decimals appear as a result of a division, they have to be kept in the calculation and they can only be removed from it by means of multiplication.

*Example*

| | | Second player enters | 65 |
|---|---|---|---|
| chooses 9 | + 9 | | |
| First player enters | 871 | | |
| First player calls 'add'; | | Chooses 7 | + |
| | ——— | | ——— |
| | 880 | | 66 |

| | 110 | Second player calls | 11 |
|---|---|---|---|
| Chooses 8 | 8/880 | 'divide'; chooses 6 | 6/66 |
| Calls 'subtract'; | 110 | | 11 |
| chooses 4 | − 4 | Chooses 5 | − |
| | ——— | | ——— |
| | 106 | | 10 |

| | 106 | Calls 'divide'; | 5 |
|---|---|---|---|
| Chooses 1 | 1/106 | chooses 2 | 2/10 |
| Calls 'add'; chooses 6 | 106 | Chooses 3 | 5 |
| | + 6 | | + |
| | ——— | | ——— |
| | 112 | | 5 |

| | 16 | Calls 'divide'; | |
|---|---|---|---|
| Chooses 7 | 7/112 | chooses 8 | 8/5 |

And so the game continues for another four rounds. If on
player reaches 0 exactly he is the winner. If neither reache
0 the winner is the one with the lowest score in terms o
digits: 4 is lower than −9 for example.

---

# Lost and Found

Here's a calculator trick with a difference. Instead of pre
dicting an answer, or telling your subject the answer to
calculator calculation after he has done all the work an
you have seen none of it, in this trick you have to show
tremendous mental skills and tell him which of the digit
in his answer he has deliberately lost.

To perform this trick, this is what you must do:

1. Give the calculator to your friend and ask him to think of a number. Tell him to enter this into the calculator.
2. Tell him to multiply by 100.
3. Tell him to add 36.
4. Tell him to subtract the number he first entered.
5. Ask him to tell you all the digits in the answer, *except* for one of them.
6. Now, in your head, add up the digits your friend has told you.
7. Work out what would be the next highest multiple of 9.
8. Now subtract the total of the digits from this multiple of 9.
9. The answer you get will be the same as the lost digit.
10. Tell your friend that you have found it, and tell him what it is.

*Example:*

| | |
|---|---:|
| Suppose that your friend entered | 493 |
| Multiply by 100 | × 100 |
| | 49300 |
| Add 36 | + 36 |
| | 49336 |

*continued*

|  | 49336 |
|---|---|
| Subtract the first number | − 493 |
|  | 48843 |

| Ask him to tell you the digits all except for one and add them in your head | 4 |
|---|---|
|  | 8 |
|  | 8 |
|  | + 4 |
|  | 24 |

|  | 2.66666• |
| Work out the next multiple of 9 by dividing 9 into 24 and taking the next whole number above your answer and multiplying that by 9 | 9/24 |
|  | 3 |
|  | × 9 |
|  | 27 |

| Now subtract the answer to your addition from this multiple of 9 and the answer will be the lost digit | 27 |
|---|---|
|  | − 24 |
|  | 3 |

In this case the lost and found digit is 3.

---

# How Old Are You?

How old are you? No, not in years! Not in months, not in days, not in hours, not in minutes, but in *seconds*! How many seconds have gone by since you were born? With your calculator you can work out the answer. Here's how:

Step 1 : Copy the list of years below. Draw a line under the year you were born and a second line above the present year. Count the number of years between the two lines you have drawn, and multiply this number by 365. Then count the

umber of Xs between the two lines, and add that number
o the calculator total.

| 1960 X | 1970 | 1980 X |
|--------|------|--------|
| 1961 | 1971 | 1981 |
| 1962 | 1972 X | 1982 |
| 1963 | 1973 | 1983 |
| 1964 X | 1974 | 1984 X |
| 1965 | 1975 | 1985 |
| 1966 | 1976 X | |
| 1967 | 1977 | |
| 1968 X | 1978 | |
| 1969 | 1979 | |

Step 2: In the list of months below find the month you
vere born in, and add the number next to it to the previous
calculator total.

| | |
|-----------|------|
| January: | 366 |
| February: | 335 |
| March: | 306 |
| April: | 275 |
| May: | 245 |
| June: | 214 |
| July: | 184 |
| August: | 153 |
| September: | 122 |
| October: | 92 |
| November: | 61 |
| December: | 31 |

Step 3: Subtract the day of the month on which you were
born.

Step 4: If you were born in January or February of any
year not marked X, subtract 1. If you were born in March
or any later month, no matter what year it was, do nothing
in this step. And if you were born at any time in any of the
years marked X, also do nothing.

Step 5: Using the new list of months below, find the present calendar month and add the number next to it to the previous total.

| | | | |
|---|---|---|---|
| January: | 0 | July: | 182 |
| February: | 31 | August: | 213 |
| March: | 60 | September: | 244 |
| April: | 91 | October: | 274 |
| May: | 121 | November: | 305 |
| June: | 152 | December: | 335 |

Step 6: If the current month is not January or February and the current year is not marked X, subtract 1. If the month is not January or February, but the year is marked X, do not subtract 1. And if the year is not marked X, but the month is January or February, again do nothing in this step.

Step 7: Add one number less than the day of the month it is today.

Step 8: Multiply by 24.

Step 9: If you do not know the time of the day you were born, add 24 to the calculator total, skip steps 9 and 10, and go on to Step 11. Your answer will not be exact, but it will still be very close. If you do know the time, take the hour you were born and find it in the list of hours below. Then add the number next to it to your calculator total.

| | | | |
|---|---|---|---|
| Midnight | 24 | 9 a.m. | 15 |
| 1 a.m. | 23 | 10 a.m. | 14 |
| 2 a.m. | 22 | 11 a.m. | 13 |
| 3 a.m. | 21 | Noon: | 12 |
| 4 a.m. | 20 | | |
| 5 a.m. | 19 | | |
| 6 a.m. | 18 | | |
| 7 a.m. | 17 | | |
| 8 a.m. | 16 | | |

| 1 p.m. | 11 | 7 p.m. | 5 |
|---|---|---|---|
| 2 p.m. | 10 | 8 p.m. | 4 |
| 3 p.m. | 9 | 9 p.m. | 3 |
| 4 p.m. | 8 | 10 p.m. | 2 |
| 5 p.m. | 7 | 11 p.m. | 1 |
| 6 p.m. | 6 | | |

**Step 10:**  See what time it is now. Again ignore the minutes. Find the hour in the list of hours below and add the number given next to it to your present calculator total.

| Midnight: | 0 | Noon: | 12 |
|---|---|---|---|
| 1 a.m. | 1 | 1 p.m. | 13 |
| 2 a.m. | 2 | 2 p.m. | 14 |
| 3 a.m. | 3 | 3 p.m. | 15 |
| 4 a.m. | 4 | 4 p.m. | 16 |
| 5 a.m. | 5 | 5 p.m. | 17 |
| 6 a.m. | 6 | 6 p.m. | 18 |
| 7 a.m. | 7 | 7 p.m. | 19 |
| 8 a.m. | 8 | 8 p.m. | 20 |
| 9 a.m. | 9 | 9 p.m. | 21 |
| 10 a.m. | 10 | 10 p.m. | 22 |
| 11 a.m. | 11 | 11 p.m. | 23 |

**Step 12:**  If you do not know the minute you were born, skip steps 12 and 13 and go on to step 14. If you do know the minute, ignore the hour, and subtract the number of minutes from the calculator total.

**Step 13:**  See what time it is. Ignoring the hour, add the minutes to the calculator total.

**Step 14:**  This is your up-to-the-minute age in minutes. To work out your age in seconds, you will have to multiply by 60. If your calculator only has an eight-digit display you can get the answer by multiplying by 6 and then writing the calculator total on paper with an extra zero at the end. So now you know the answer, how does it feel to be millions of seconds old?

# Date Jumbler

Calculators have a wonderful way of producing unexpected numbers from what appears to be a complete jumble of sums. In this case, your calculator will give you an answer which not only starts with the number you first entered into it, but which ends with the date of the day on which you are doing the calculation.

This is how it works:

1. Pick any five-digit number at random and enter this into your calculator.
2. Multiply this number by 2.
3. Add 5.
4. Now multiply this total by 50.
5. Add the date (the number of the day in the month).
6. Add the number of days in a year (365), an ordinary year in this case, not a leap year.
7. Subtract 615 from the total on the calculator screen.
8. Look at the answer on the calculator screen. You will see that there are seven digits. The first five will be the five digits in your original number. The last two will be the same as the date.

9. Your calculator has taken all these jumbled sums and produced another brilliant result!

*Example:*

Imagine that you start with a five-digit number like:

| | | |
|---|---:|---:|
| | | 24680 |
| Multiply it by 2 | 24680 | |
| | × 2 | |
| | 49360 | |
| Add 5 | + 5 | |
| | 49365 | |
| Multiply by 50 | × 50 | |
| | 2468250 | |
| Add the date 21 | + 21 | |
| | 2468271 | |
| Add 365 | + 365 | |
| | 2468636 | |
| Subtract 615 | − 615 | |
| | 2468021 | |

The first five digits are the same as the original number, and the last two are the same as the date.

---

# Calculator Codes

Elsewhere in the book you can read about using your calculator to write words for you. But here is another way in which you can use your calculator to express words. This time you use a code. The code is based on giving a number to each letter of the alphabet from A to Z. There are twenty-six letters in the alphabet, so numbering them from 1 to 26, the code looks like this:

| | | |
|---|---|---|
| A = 1 | I = 9 | S = 19 |
| B = 2 | J = 10 | T = 20 |
| C = 3 | K = 11 | U = 21 |
| D = 4 | L = 12 | V = 22 |
| E = 5 | M = 13 | W = 23 |
| F = 6 | N = 14 | X = 24 |
| G = 7 | O = 15 | Y = 25 |
| H = 8 | P = 16 | Z = 26 |
| | Q = 17 | |
| | R = 18 | |

Once you have copied out the code, you can use it to send messages to anyone else who also has a copy of it.

If you wanted to send the message:

COME ROUND TO MY HOUSE FOR TEA

You would write it in code like this:

3 15 13 5 / 18 15 21 14 4 / 20 15 / 13 25 / 8 15 21 19 5 / 6 15 18 / 20 5 1

Apart from using the code to send messages, you can use it to play an interesting game. The object of this game is to find the word which contains the letters that when written as numbers and MULTIPLIED together gives you the highest eight-digit total that you can get on your calculator. This means of course the one nearest to 99,999,999. (Any number higher than that causes the calculator overflow sign to flash on.)

Look at this example before you try to find the word yourself:

Start with an easy word: YACHT
Written in code it is 25 1 3 8 20
Written with multiplication signs as a sum it is:

$$25 \times 1 \times 3 \times 8 \times 20$$

and the answer is :

$$
\begin{array}{r}
25 \\
\times\ 1 \\
\hline
25 \\
\times\ 3 \\
\hline
75 \\
\times\ 8 \\
\hline
600 \\
\times\ 20 \\
\hline
12000
\end{array}
$$

But 12,000 is a long way short of 99,999,999.
So you have to find a word with a lot of high numbered letters, but not so many that their total goes over 100,000,000.
Alternatively, find a longer word with lower scoring letters.

The choice is very wide indeed. Have fun!

---

# Sprinting to One Hundred

The object of this game is to reach 100 before your opponent.

To play the game you will need :

    2 players
    2 calculators
    2 sheets of paper
    2 pencils

You play the game like this :

1. Both players enter any digit they like into their calculators.
2. They also write down another digit *in secret*.
3. Toss a coin to see who will start.
4. The first player gives the other any one of the four

mathematical functions to perform with his secret
number.

5. The second player makes this calculation and then tells
   the first player which mathematical function he must
   perform with his secret number.

6. The play continues in this way, with each player writing
   down a secret number after each turn.

7. The first player to get 100 on the screen is the winner.

*Example:*

| Player A | Player B |
|---|---|
| Enters 8 | Enters 6 |
| Writes down 5 | Writes down 3 |
| Tells B to add | |

$$\begin{array}{r} 6 \\ + 3 \\ \hline 9 \end{array}$$

$$\begin{array}{r} 8 \\ \times\ 5 \\ \hline 40 \end{array}$$

Tells A to multiply
Writes down 4

Writes down 9
Tells B to multiply

$$\begin{array}{r} 9 \\ \times\ 4 \\ \hline 36 \end{array}$$

$$\begin{array}{l} 4.444\bullet \\ 9\,\overline{)40} \end{array}$$

Writes down 6
Tells B to subtract

Writes down 7
Tells A to divide

$$\begin{array}{r} 36 \\ - 7 \\ \hline 29 \end{array}$$

$$\begin{array}{r} 4.444\bullet \\ \times\ 6 \\ \hline 26.666\bullet \end{array}$$

Writes down 5
Tells A to multiply

Etcetera!

110

# Puzzle Answers

*Fill-in Puzzles (Page 26)*

The sequence should be filled in to look like these:

a.
$$1 \times 9 + 2 = 11$$
$$12 \times 9 + 3 = 111$$
$$123 \times 9 + 4 = 1111$$
$$1234 \times 9 + 5 = 11111$$
$$12345 \times 9 + 6 = 111111$$
$$123456 \times 9 + 7 = 1111111$$
$$1234567 \times 9 + 8 = 11111111$$
$$12345678 \times 9 + 9 = 111111111$$

b.
$$1 \times 9 - 1 = 8$$
$$21 \times 9 - 1 = 188$$
$$321 \times 9 - 1 = 2888$$
$$4321 \times 9 - 1 = 38888$$
$$54321 \times 9 - 1 = 488888$$
$$654321 \times 9 - 1 = 5888888$$
$$7654321 \times 9 - 1 = 68888888$$
$$87654321 \times 9 - 1 = 788888888$$
$$987654321 \times 9 - 1 = 8888888888$$

c.
$$12345679 \times 9 = 111111111$$
$$12345679 \times 18 = 222222222$$
$$12345679 \times 27 = 333333333$$
$$12345679 \times 36 = 444444444$$
$$12345679 \times 45 = 555555555$$
$$12345679 \times 54 = 666666666$$
$$12345679 \times 63 = 777777777$$
$$12345679 \times 72 = 888888888$$
$$12345679 \times 81 = 999999999$$

The multipliers are all multiples of 9, aren't they?

d.
$$9 \times 9 + 7 = 88$$
$$98 \times 9 + 6 = 888$$
$$987 \times 9 + 5 = 8888$$
$$9876 \times 9 + 4 = 88888$$
$$98765 \times 9 + 3 = 888888$$
$$987654 \times 9 + 2 = 8888888$$
$$9876543 \times 9 + 1 = 88888888$$
$$98765432 \times 9 + 0 = 888888888$$

---

*Multiplication Puzzles (Page 38)*

a.   The answers should be:

3784
3159
1395
1827
2187
1435

In all the sums the digits in the answers are exactly the same as the digits in the two multipliers.

114

b.  The answers should be:

$$
\begin{array}{r}
7852 \\
5346 \\
6952 \\
7632 \\
5796
\end{array}
$$

c.  The answers should be:

$$1 \times 91 = \phantom{0}91$$
$$2 \times 91 = 182$$
$$3 \times 91 = 273$$
$$4 \times 91 = 364$$
$$5 \times 91 = 455$$
$$6 \times 91 = 546$$
$$7 \times 91 = 637$$
$$8 \times 91 = 728$$
$$9 \times 91 = 819$$

The last digit in each answer is the same as the first digit in the following answer.
If you add the digits in each answer you will get a sequence of numbers from 10 to 18.

d.  There are two answers to this question:
One is 39157        39 1 57

$$
\begin{array}{r}
39 \\
\times\ 57 \\
\hline
2223 \\
-\ 1 \\
\hline
2222
\end{array}
$$

The other is 57139    57 1 39

$$
\begin{array}{r}
57 \\
\times\ 39 \\
\hline
2223 \\
-\ 1 \\
\hline
2222 \\
\end{array}
$$

---

*All Digit Puzzles (Page 48)*

a.  Some other addition sums that use all the digits from 1 to 9 are:

$$
\begin{array}{r}
146 \\
+\ 583 \\
\hline
729 \\
\end{array}
\qquad
\begin{array}{r}
341 \\
+\ 586 \\
\hline
927 \\
\end{array}
$$

$$
\begin{array}{r}
216 \\
+\ 738 \\
\hline
954 \\
\end{array}
\qquad
\begin{array}{r}
216 \\
+\ 748 \\
\hline
963 \\
\end{array}
$$

There are still others which you have probably found for yourself. Well done!

IT WAS NOTHING – ANY GENIUS COULD DO IT!

b. There are lots of different ways in which you can write these sums. Here are a couple of the ones you might have found:

```
     1                AND:              1
   + 2                              + (2 × 3) = 6
   ───                              ────
    (3)                               (7)
   + 3                              + (4 × 5) = 20
   ───                              ────
    (6)                              (27)
   + 4                              − 6
   ───                              ────
   (10)                             (21)
   + 5                              + 7
   ───                              ────
   (15)                             (28)
   + 6                              + (8 × 9 = 72
   ───                              ────
   (21)                             100
   + 7
   ───
   (28)
 + (8 × 9) = 72
   ─────
   (28)
 + 72
   ───
   100
```

117

c. The two numbers you should end up with are:

$$6792$$
$$\text{and} \quad 13584$$

Multiply the smaller by 2 to check that the other is double it:

$$
\begin{array}{r}
6792 \\
\times\ 2 \\
\hline
13584
\end{array}
$$

d. There are several different sums that you can make using all the digits on your calculator. These are some of them:

$$
\begin{array}{r}
157 \\
\times\ 28 \\
\hline
4396
\end{array}
\qquad
\begin{array}{r}
715 \\
\times\ 46 \\
\hline
32890
\end{array}
\qquad
\begin{array}{r}
367 \\
\times\ 52 \\
\hline
19084
\end{array}
\qquad
\begin{array}{r}
297 \\
\times\ 18 \\
\hline
5346
\end{array}
\qquad
\begin{array}{r}
402 \\
\times\ 39 \\
\hline
15678
\end{array}
$$

---

## Mixed Puzzles 1 (Page 60)

a. No matter which line of digits you use, the answer to the addition will always be 1,110. The reason for this is that the digits at either end of the line add up to 10 and therefore they will be units in one direction and hundreds in the other. The two fives also add up to ten and they will occur in the middle. So the answer will always be 1,110.

b. The digits in your answers will always add up to 18. For example:

$$
\begin{array}{r}
99 \\
\times\ 89 \\
\hline
8811
\end{array}
\qquad \text{AND:} \qquad
\begin{array}{r}
8 \\
8 \\
1 \\
+\ 1 \\
\hline
18
\end{array}
$$

118

You can make eight 8's add up to 1,000 like this:

$$
\begin{array}{r}
8 \\
8 \\
8 \\
88 \\
888 \\
\hline
1000
\end{array}
$$

The answer to this question is simply 4!
Watch:

$$
\begin{array}{r}
4 \\
+ 8 \\
\hline
12 \\
- 8 \\
\hline
4 \\
\times 8 \\
\hline
\end{array}
$$

$$32 \div 8 \quad 8\overline{)32} \; {}^{4}$$

and 4 is in fact the number you began with!

The number should be 4368.
This is four digits long.
The last digit 8 is double the first digit 4.
The second digit 3 is three less than the third digit 6.
And the sum of the first digit and the last digit 4 + 8 = 12
is twice the third digit: 2 × 6 = 12.

f.   The digits from 1 to 7 should be arranged like this:

$$
\begin{array}{r}
1 \\
2 \\
34 \\
56 \\
+\ 7 \\
\hline
100 \\
\end{array}
$$

g.   The three digits are 1.25:

$$
\begin{array}{r}
1.25 \\
\times\ 4 \\
\hline
5.00 \\
\end{array}
$$

h.   The sum you enter into your calculator should look like this:

$$(0.5 \times 0.5) \div 0.5 = 0.5$$

or:

$$
\begin{array}{r}
0.5 \\
\times\ 0.5 \\
\hline
\end{array}
$$

$$
0.25 \div 0.5 \overline{)0.25} \ \ ^{0.5}
$$

---

*Some Sum! (Page 71)*

1.   1066 × 13            = 13858
2.   13858 × 366          = 5072028
3.   5072028 − 28         = 5072000.
4.   5072000 ÷ 1000       = 5072
5.   5072 − 6             = 5066
6.   5066 − 1066          = 4000
7.   4000 ÷ 100           = 40
8.   40 − 39              = 1

---

a.  The complete sequence should look like this:

$$33 \times 3367 = 111111$$
$$66 \times 3367 = 222222$$
$$99 \times 3367 = 333333$$
$$132 \times 3367 = 444444$$
$$165 \times 3367 = 555555$$
$$198 \times 3367 = 666666$$
$$231 \times 3367 = 777777$$
$$264 \times 3367 = 888888$$
$$297 \times 3367 = 999999$$

b.  The two numbers are 7 and 1:

$$\begin{array}{r} 7 \\ \times\ 1 \\ \hline 7 \end{array}$$

c.  The three consecutive numbers are 8, 9, and 10:

$$\begin{array}{r} 8 \\ 9 \\ +\ 10 \\ \hline 27 \end{array}$$

d.  On an eight-digit calculator the highest number you can show is 99,999,999. Since you can show every whole number below that, the answer must be that you can show the impressive total of ninety-nine million, nine hundred and ninety-nine thousand, nine hundred and ninety-nine whole numbers.

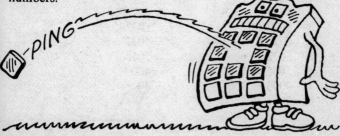

e.  The completed sequence should look like this:

$$15873 \times 7 = 111111$$
$$15873 \times 14 = 222222$$
$$15873 \times 21 = 333333$$
$$15873 \times 28 = 444444$$
$$15873 \times 35 = 555555$$
$$15873 \times 42 = 666666$$
$$15873 \times 49 = 777777$$
$$15873 \times 56 = 888888$$
$$18573 \times 63 = 999999$$

f.  The completed sequence should look like this:

$$1 \times 8 + 1 = 9$$
$$12 \times 8 + 2 = 98$$
$$123 \times 8 + 3 = 987$$
$$1234 \times 8 + 4 = 9876$$
$$12345 \times 8 + 5 = 98765$$
$$123456 \times 8 + 6 = 987654$$
$$1234567 \times 8 + 7 = 9876543$$
$$12345678 \times 8 + 8 = 98765432$$

# Armada Crossword Books

compiled by Robert Newton

Are you a clued-up quizzler? Can you solve cunning clues quick as a flash? Here are sixteen terrific collections of 100 crosswords specially compiled for Armada. Pick up a pencil and fill in the answers!

*And* there's the extra game of clues and anagrams – **Starwords** – to add to the fun!

Armada

# THE AWFUL JOKE BOOK

*compiled by Mary Danby*

The best of the worst! Here is a great new
collection of ghastly gags, hideous howlers,
riotous riddles and witty wisecracks –
illustrated with scores of hilarious cartoons.
You'll drive your family and friends
round the bend! Here are a couple of
examples . . .

What is the main ingredient in dog biscuits?
*Collie flour*.

NEW COWHAND: What is the name of this ranch?
RANCHER: The Lazy G Triple Diamond Circle S
    Bar Z.
NEW COWHAND: How many head of cattle are there?
RANCHER: Not many. Only a few of them survive the
    branding.

**Armada**

# THE EXPLORER'S HANDBOOK

Peter Eldin

What to do when you're on safari, up the Pole, on the rocks, up the creek, under the weather, up a gum-tree, in deep water, or simply high and dry . . .

Here's how to –

Signal with a Saucepan
Build an Igloo
Eat with Chopsticks
Escape from a Shark
Get on with a Camel

and many more ways to survive off the beaten track!

Armada

# THE SECRET AGENT'S HANDBOOK

Peter Eldin

A guide for sleuths, spies and private eyes . . .

Here's the low-down on –

Coded Messages

Secret Handshakes

Disguises

Passwords

Spy Traps

Agents' Language

Invisible Writing

The Toothpaste Hideout

and many more highly confidential instructions on how to become a Top Secret Agent.

Armada

## has a whole shipload
## of exciting books for you

Armadas are chosen by children all over the world. They're designed to fit your pocket, and your pocket money too. They're colourful, exciting, and there are hundreds of titles to choose from. Armada has something for everyone:

Mystery and adventure series to collect, with favourite characters and authors ... like Alfred Hitchcock and The Three Investigators – the Hardy Boys – young detective Nancy Drew – the intrepid Lone Piners – Biggles – the rascally William – and others.

Hair-raising Spinechillers – Ghost, Monster and Science Fiction stories. Fascinating quiz and puzzle books. Exciting hobby books. Lots of hilarious fun books. Many famous stories. Thrilling pony adventures. Popular school stories – and many more.

You can build up your own Armada collection – and new Armadas are published every month, so look out for the latest additions to the Captain's cargo.

Armadas are available in bookshops and newsagents.

Armada